T0159244

Black Africa

Cheikh Anta Diop

BLACK AFRICA

*The Economic and Cultural Basis
for a Federated State*

**Translated by
Harold J. Salemson**

AFRICA WORLD PRESS EDITION

LAWRENCE HILL BOOKS

Library of Congress Cataloging-in-Publication Data

Diop, Cheikh Anta.
  Black Africa : the economic and cultural basis for
a federated state.
  Translation of : Les fondements économique et
culturels d'un état fédéral d'Afrique noire.
  Bibliography: p. 90
    1. Africa, Sub-Saharan—Economic conditions.
2. Africa, Sub-Saharan—Civilization. 3. Pan-Africanism.
4. Africa, Sub-Saharan—Politics and government.
5. Africa, Sub-Saharan—Industries. 6. Power resources—
Africa, Sub-Saharan. I. Title.
HC800.D5613 1987   330.967   87-17704
ISBN 978-1-55652-061-7, previously 0-88208-223-X
ISBN 0-86543-058-6 (Africa World Press)

This revised edition jointly published 1987
by Lawrence Hill Books
an imprint of Chicago Review Press, Incorporated
814 North Franklin Street
Chicago, Illinois 60610
ISBN 978-1-55652-061-7
and Africa World Press, Inc., PO Box 1892, Trenton, NJ, 08608

Printed in the United States of America

Table of Contents

Hydraulic Energy; Solar Energy; Atomic Energy; Thermonuclear Energy; Wind Energy; Thermal Energy of the Seas; Tidal Energy; Global Heat; Volcanic Thermal Energy and Geothermal Energy.

Part III

The Zaire River Basin; The Gulf of Benin Region; Ghana and the Ivory Coast; Guinea, Sierra Leone, Liberia; Tropical Zone (Senegal, Mali, Niger); Nilotic Sudan, Great Lakes, Ethiopia; Zambezi River Basin; Union of South Africa; Transport; Training Key Personnel.

Conclusion

Foreword to the English Edition

Since 1960, when the first edition of this work appeared, the specter of South-Americanization that should have been staved off has instead materialized everywhere. African unity has made only limited progress in certain specific domains of economic, cultural, academic or other life. Even in those cases, we have had only regional or continental groupings, never involving any real surrender of an iota of national sovereignty and, therefore, not irreversible. They include: OERS (Organisation des Etats Riverains du fleuve Sénégal; Organization of States Bordering the Senegal River); UDEAC (*Union Douanière des Etats de l'Afrique Centrale;* Customs Union of Central African States); OERM (*Organisation Economique de la Région du Maghreb;* Economic Organization of North Africa); EACM (East African Community and Common Market; CEAO (*Communauté Economique de l'Afrique de l'Ouest;* West African Economic Community); CEDEAO (*Communauté Economique des Etats de l'Afrique de l'Ouest;* The Economic Community of West African States).

Most of these groupings died as they were born, about one every two years. Such was the case with the Union of East Africa (including Kenya, Tanzania and Uganda), which had given rise to so many hopes.

The CEAO (including Senegal, Niger, Ivory Coast, Mali, Mauritania, Upper Volta, Togo and Benin) and CEDEAO (Nigeria, Ivory Coast, Mali, Senegal, Upper Volta, Niger, Togo, Guinea and Sierra Leone) are recent creations in West Africa but no less fragile. All of them are giants with feet of clay engaged in trying to square the circle: to achieve meaningful economic unity without political union. No one wants to make the necessary sacrifice to achieve political unity. All hope to gain the benefits of economic integration without sacrificing the selfish interests of their governing groups on the altar of African unity. That is the fundamental contradiction lying at the base of all these ephemeral constructions and unions.

The subsidiaries of multinational companies established in the countries making up the so-called Union (whether CEAO or CEDEAO) will without difficulty get around the protective laws that have so laboriously been passed. For instance, within the CEAO Senegal and the Ivory Coast harbor most of the subsidiaries of foreign companies there to manufacture cheaply and to export to the rest of the West African zone. These two countries have not used the definition of a national company that other, less-industrialized nations have, such as Mali, Niger, Upper Volta and Mauritania. Whereas Senegal held that even a foreign-financed company operating within the CEAO must be considered a national company if it brought a 75 percent transformation to a homegrown product, the other partners were concerned with the company's origin, the ownership of its capital and the ultimate destination of its profits and, therefore, demanded a better definition of the concept of national companies.

The Organization of African Unity is better than nothing. If only its authority were stronger, if a determinate part of the sovereignty of the various states were transferred to it in specific domains, it would play a more efficacious role. At the moment, this would seem especially necessary in the matter of defense in order to counter the South African peril. Both Pretoria and Israel now possess the atomic bomb without having had to carry out their own nuclear explosions, thanks to Western duplicity.

Let the African peoples not be misled. The nuclear test in the Kalahari that Pretoria recently postponed does not mean it has given up on atomic weapons: it has them already. The test had been intended mainly to intimidate the African states. It was to have been a shattering way of letting them know that Pretoria had joined the atomic club.

Tomorrow, or in ten years, the German rockets that the OTRAG (Orbital Transport und Raketen Aktion Gesellschaft) Company is beginning to manufacture in Equatorial Africa will be able to deliver Pretoria's nuclear warheads with amazing precision. This will allow South Africa to have the entire Black Continent at its mercy— before Nigeria or Zaïre are aroused or become sufficiently effective.

We may hope that there might yet come into being an international solidarity of peoples to preclude such genocide; demographic pressure is at present the only "atomic weapon of Black Africa."

One is deeply disturbed to read such lines as:

> Plans formulated in the United States in 1970 to control birth rates are extremely far-reaching and suggest, for example, the idea of putting sterilizing agents into the water supply of cities or household salt, if need be over the objections of local governments.[1]

On another level, in this era of energy crisis there is good reason to redefine what ought to be Africa's energy doctrine, for that action in itself will show that this book, written long before the crisis came into existence, foretold it.

Toward an African Energy Doctrine

The days of the nineteenth-century dwarf states are gone. Our main security and development problems can be solved only on a continental scale and preferably within a federal framework.

Let us just take one example among many to illustrate this

idea. What is the meaning of the rights granted under the Law of the Sea to such tiny landlocked or semiarid states as Rwanda, Burundi, Zambia, Niger, Chad, Upper Volta or the Central African Empire? Within two generations, a good share of the customary materials indispensable to our daily lives (including iron, aluminum, copper, uranium, zinc, manganese and cobalt) will have completely disappeared from land areas. Suitable technical equipment will be required to extract them from ocean bottoms exceeding two thousand meters (a mile and a quarter). A right which one has no material or technical way of using is just a dead letter. How would states barely as large as one section of Paris or New York—even if their populations grew—be able to run the risk of sending expeditions on their own into the abyssal depths to secure urgently needed supplies of raw materials? It would be just as easy for a legless man to compete in races at the Olympic Games. An African Kuwait, such as Gabon, in less than sixty years will be an empty shell.

Enlightened self-interest itself argues for the adoption, before it is too late, of a federal system. Belgian-American interests, preparing for the political instability that would prevail in the colonies following World War II, working at maximum rates and beyond, mined all the uranium of the then Belgian Congo in less than ten years and stockpiled it at Oolen in Belgium. The Shinrolowbe mines in Zaïre today are emptied, having supplied the major part of the uranium that went into the Nagasaki and Hiroshima bombs. Until 1952, Zaïre was the world's leading uranium producer; now it ranks sixteenth in reserves and has ceased to be counted among the producers. This one example shows how fast our continent can have its nonrenewable treasures sucked away while we nap.

The upshot is that only a continentwide or a subcontinentwide federated state can offer a safe political and economic area, stable enough for a rational formula covering the development of our countries with their infinitely varied potentials to be put into effect. Because the federated state involves a real surrender of sovereignty, it is an irreversible structure that has nothing in common with the transitory economic groupings that have proliferated since independence.

Within a federated state, today's political boundaries would become mere local administrative lines, and disagreements—such as the ones which have pitted or presently pit Mali against Upper Volta, Ghana against Togo, Libya against Chad, Morocco against Mauritania in the Polisario, Somalia against Ethiopia—would no longer be conceivable. That, therefore, is the framework within which we have chosen to deal with Africa's energy problems.

The ideas presented in popular form in this work, which was first written in 1960 before the world energy crisis, are topical. In fact, it includes the whole of today's OMVS (L'Organisation pour la Mise en Valeur du [Fleuve] Sénégal; The Organization for the Development of the River Senegal) program, before the fact.

We would like in these prefatory pages to indicate how we conceive an African Energy Doctrine. What we are proposing is a schema of continentwide energy development that takes into account at one and the same time renewable and nonrenewable energy resources, ecology and the technical advances of the coming decades.

From such a starting point we will try to establish not only on the historical/cultural level but also on that of economic rationality a future African-Arab cooperation in the particular sphere of use of energy resources.

Black Africa will have to find a formula of energy pluralism that harmoniously combines utilization of the following sources of energy: 1) hydroelectric energy (dams); 2) solar energy; 3) nuclear energy; 4) geothermal energy; 5) hydrocarbons (petroleum); and 6) thermonuclear energy.

The first five sources of energy are already utilizable to various degrees in Africa and the rest of the world, while the last has not reached a practically operable stage. There can be no doubt, despite a requisite degree of pessimism, that its applications will become operational within the next forty years—that is, in less than two generations—at the very moment when the reign of oil will be ending with the exhaustion of the last deposits on earth. We cannot here go into technical aspects of the problems; that would make no sense in a text which aims to popularize ideas that are vital to us all. However, if that source of energy were to become available, with effective control of thermonuclear reactions, the energy needs of the planet would be answered for a period of a billion—repeat, one billion—years. The future instruments that produce this energy, whether called thermonuclear reactors or tokomaks (from the Soviet origin of the first experimental prototypes so named), will be fed in their final and truly operational stages by heavy hydrogen, obtained basically through the electrolysis of sea water.

Every country would be able to have its own electrolytic setup which would be more than enough to handle its current needs. But if energy consumption were to increase indefinitely, African dams would be the proper installations for the production of heavy hydrogen by way of electrolysis; at the same time they would supply ordinary hydrogen for stockpiling as eventual replacement for gasoline to fuel a type of internal-combustion engine to be invented.

As far as solar energy is concerned, ongoing research with a view to reducing the cost of solar cells will perhaps allow us on the threshold of the year 2000 to have operational solar powerplants, known as land or space heliovoltaics. We stated in this work that the practical application of solar energy for industry was basically a problem of physical chemistry; events have not proved us wrong. Nevertheless, solar technology is improving daily, and the application of solar energy to home heating and cooling is well under way. Solar energy has already been put to use in a number of high-rise buildings, and communal solar receptors are in operation.

For a great many reasons which would be difficult to detail here we believe that the continentwide options available to Africa should be the following: first, to bank on the triumph of thermonuclear energy and immediately create a pilot fusion center in an appropriate African country, open to all qualified African researchers willing to follow this line of pursuit; fusion is only very slightly polluting, either radioactively or thermally[2]; second, to bank supplementarily on solar energy; in the third place to bank on geothermal energy (also producing only slight pollution), especially for the volcanic regions of East Africa.

There is no need here to go into the sources of wind, tidal or other energy which, while less significant, are discussed in the text proper.

The three abovementioned sources (thermonuclear, solar and geothermal) now being domesticated fall into place with three others that are already standard: hydroelectricity (dams); nuclear fission, as opposed to the nuclear fusion just considered; and hydrocarbons.

The intensification of petroleum prospecting each year improves Africa's posture in the realm of hydrocarbons, but it is well known that these are highly polluting and are now being depleted throughout the world. Taking these two factors into account, as well as the imminent arrival of new sources of energy, one can anticipate that hydrocarbons will increasingly be considered only as raw materials for the synthetic chemical industry.

As for nuclear fission, it is regrettable that the political historical context no longer allows us a choice. We are obliged to develop this highly polluting technology on the African continent, because our peoples' survival depends upon it. We will have to opt for second-generation reactors (that is, breeders or superregenerators), which at their operational stage with all the dangers involved produce more fuel than they consume—as is well known.

The seismic stability of the African continent will allow stockpiling of atomic wastes until a valid efficient method of disposing of these may be found, instead of embedding them in concrete or sinking them in the ocean by pipeline, as some of the great powers with Atlantic seacoasts, such as Great Britain, have been doing.

Finally, hydroelectric power today is the principal source of energy for sub-Saharan Africa. Let us not forget that in colonial days the Belgians had already calculated that equipping the Inga site on the Zaïre River would have been enough to supply all the African energy needs of that day—or to light the entire continent of South America. They at one time considered transporting this power in direct current (because there is less loss) from the Equator to Spain, Portugal and Italy and selling it to power-poor southern Europe. Their calculations showed that it could be sold in Europe at a competitive price per kilowatt, even after having been transported over so long a distance.

Abundant hydroelectric power has allowed Zaïre to undertake the installation of a plant for the enrichment of uranium, a technique requiring vast amounts of electricity.

We might also point to the dams at Kaborabassa, Aawan and elsewhere. Two-thirds of the world's reserves of hydro-electric power are concentrated in Africa.

Black Africa is, therefore, a continent rich in power. Equipping the present sites and connecting them in an African grid would permit the creation of an integrated continentwide electrical-energy market, covering virtually all the energy needs of the African states through rational distribution without waste. The interconnection of grids is so rational a solution that even countries with different economic systems resort to it. Certain Soviet purchases in Europe, namely, in West Germany, are paid for with electric power, or can be considered to be.

Establishment of the African grid would allow for power from Zaïre to be delivered even to the edges of the desert and, thus, keep the latter from spreading.

At this time, the longest powerline for electrical energy in direct current in the world is being built in Zaïre, between Kinshasa and the Shaba, a distance of 2,000 kilometers. Another line of the same type built by the Portuguese is unfortunately still in operation, between Kaborabassa (Mozambique) and Johannesburg, supplying power to Pretoria's factories of death. We are convinced that the Mozambican authorities will do their utmost to put an end to this as soon as possible.

A private organization, the UPDEA (*Union des Producteurs et des Distributeurs d'Electricité en Afrique;* Union of African Producers and Distributors of Electricity) has been set up in the past few years and is at work to complete the grid. The pitfalls of such a solution are evident. The ideal would be for problems as vital as this to be taken in hand by a continentwide federated state rather than by a foreign financial group. All deviations are conceivable!

We can also understand that such is the prerequisite for self-centered development—as economists employ that term when they emphasize this kind of development—and add that it is possible only by throwing off the (iniquitous) conditions of the international marketplace and making a break for as long as necessary with that kind of system, as was done, for example, by the Soviet Union or China. Economists have never spelled out the conditions that make such a withdrawal possible; this cannot be held against them, for such a definition is outside the framework of economics. Only a continentwide or subcontinentwide federated state can permit realization of such self-centered development.

Bases for African-Arab Cooperation

I have demonstrated in my earlier books all the biological and cultural kinship between Arabs and Black Africans, a kinship so old that it goes back to the fifth millennium BC and the beginning of the fourth with the birth of the Semitic world. I further explored the "genetic kinship between Pharaonic Egyptian and the African languages" within the framework of a chapter on "The Process of Semiticization." This kinship greatly antedates Islam, but all the prejudices inherited during the history of the intervening centuries have obscured it. One day it will come to the fore once again, and it is a factor not to be overlooked in the unifying dynamic of the continent.

These historic reasons are further supported by current reasons which belong to the complementary nature of our economies in the light of the coming depletion of hydrocarbon fossil fuels.

The form of energy eventually replacing oil in the semiarid Middle East will not be nuclear fission, for fissionable resources from the earth will give out at about the time petroleum supplies are depleted—to say nothing of the special inconvenience represented by a nuclear powerplant existing beyond its use. The substitute energy will very probably be thermonuclear, that is, from nuclear fusion, or else solar. We have seen that, if this is the case, Black Africa with its hydroelectric installations might be the inexhaustible source both for heavy hydrogen, which is the raw material for thermonuclear reactors, and for the future vector of energy (i.e., the means of stockpiling and transporting) which is ordinary hydrogen. Hydrogen-fueled automobiles will necessarily replace today's gasoline-fueled vehicles. The solar car, built with photocells, will undoubtedly also come into existence, but it may be less practical because of the alternation of days and nights, even after the problem of conversion and stockpiling of solar energy is solved. It may be that the photosynthesis reaction creating hydrogen from sunlight—accomplished in laboratory experiments by the Japanese—will soon become a practical reality.

With the future appearance of hydrogen as the energy vector, a whole new technology of internal-combustion engines and various other types of motors must come into existence. It is in terms of that not-so-distant future that we must rethink all of our developmental problems in order to avoid absurd choices that might condemn the next generation—today's sixteen-year-olds—to face the worst kinds of difficulties tomorrow.

March 10, 1978

---

[1] Albert Sauvy, *La Population.* Paris: Presses universitaires de France ("Que sais-je?" Collection), 1975, p. 118.

[2] See the author's report to the PNUD (*Le Programme des Nations Unies pour le Développement;* United Nations Development Program) Ref. DP/TCDC/RAF/11, September 10, 1976, p. 68: "Technical Cooperation among African Countries."

Introduction

Our ideologists have not succeeded in moving revolutionary theory forward by one step in Black Africa. Indeed, though one be armed with so fecund a scientific method of analysis as Marxist dialectics (assuming it had been sufficiently assimilated), it would be hopeless to try to apply it to a reality of which one is totally ignorant. For a long time many of our compatriots have thought they could get by without any deep knowledge of African society and Africa in all aspects: history, languages, ethnicities, energy potential, raw materials, and the like. The conclusions reached have often been abysmally banal, when not plain and simply wrong. They have thought they could make up for the lack of ideas, breath, and revolutionary perspectives by the use of offensive, excessive, and murky vocabulary; they forgot that the truly revolutionary quality of language is its demonstrative clarity based on the objective use of facts and their dialectical relationships, which results in irresistibly convincing the intelligent reader.

In February, 1952, when I was Secretary General of the Democratic African Rally of Students, we posed the problem of the political independence of the Black Continent and the creation of a future Federated State in an article entitled "Toward a Political Ideology in Black Africa."[1] This article, which was in fact but a foreshadowing of my *The African Origin of Civilization: Myth or Reality*,[2] considered political, linguistic, historical, social, and other aspects of the question.

At that time, apart from the Malagasy deputies and the Cameroonian leader Ruben Um Nyobé, there were certainly no French-speaking Black African politicians who dared to voice the concepts of African nations, independence, or, let's face it, culture. Today's after-the-fact statements endorsing such ideas are almost frauds; at the least they are bare-faced misrepresentations.

It would be illuminating to trace the history of the actual positive use (not just as trial balloons to be shot down) of these concepts by the "fathers" of African independence, even if the use preceded their writings.

If the priorities indicated in this book had been taken into consideration in due time, especially insofar as hydroelectric development was concerned, Black Africa today would have nothing to fear from the economic problems created by the oil crisis and the drought.

A rational industrialization program would consist first of all of harnessing the immense sources of energy which nature has given to Africa and thus making possible the whole process of development: In the beginning is energy; all else flows therefrom. While exploitation of such abundant energy might become a marketing challenge for private corporations, to a developing country which must stimulate manifold activities and bring into being the apparatus needed for its emergence into the industrial era, the idea of excess energy is pure nonsense.

---

[1]"Vers une idéologie politique en Afrique Noire," in *La Voix de l'Afrique Noire* (official organ of the Étudiants du Rassemblement Démocratique Africain), February, 1952.

[2]Westport, Connecticut: Lawrence Hill & Company, 1974, a translation by Mercer Cook of *Nations nègres et culture* (1955) and selected parts of *Antériorité des civilisations nègres: Mythe ou Vérité historique?* (1967), both published by Présence Africaine, Paris.

Part I

Historical Unity: The Restoration Of African Historical Consciousness

The time has come to draw practical conclusions from years of studying African problems, to sum them up in formulas that are as clear as possible and easy to apply.

Chapter One
Origins and History of the Black World

In all likelihood, present-day African peoples are in no way invaders come from another continent; they are the aborigines. Recent scientific discoveries that show Africa to be the cradle of humanity increasingly negate the hypothesis of this continent being peopled by outlanders.

From the appearance of *homo sapiens*—from earliest prehistory until our time—we are able to trace our origins as a people without significant breaks in continuity. In early prehistory, a great South-North movement brought the African peoples of the Great Lakes region into the Nile Basin. They lived there in clusters for millennia.

In prehistoric times, it was they who created the Nilotic Sudanese civilization and what we know as Egypt.

These first Black civilizations were the first civilizations in the world, the development of Europe having been held back by the last Ice Age, a matter of a hundred thousand years.

Beginning in the sixth century BC (525, when Cambyses occupied Egypt) with the end of the independence of the great Black power base, the African peoples, until then drawn to the Nile Valley as by a magnet, fanned out over the continent. Perhaps they then came upon small pockets of populations descended from paleolithic or neolithic infiltrations.

A few centures later, around the first century, they founded the first of the continental civilizations in the West and South: Ghana, Nok-Ifé, Zimbabwe and others.

We now know, thanks to radiocarbon methods, that the earliest sites in Zimbabwe do date back at least as far as the

first century of the Christian Era. On the east coast of Africa
Roman coins have been discovered at the port of Dunford as
well as in Zanzibar, indicating a flourishing sea trade.

The first Nigerian civilization, which Bernard and William
Fagg named the Nok civilization, has been traced back to the
first millennium BC, the ceramics found there being
radiocarbon-dated over a range from 900 BC to 200 AD. The
Tarikh es-Sudan tells us that the city of Kukia, on the Niger,
former capital of Songhay before Gao, was contemporaneous
with the time of the pharaohs. However that may be, we do
know with certainty that in the eighth century AD the Empire of Ghana was already in existence, extending over all of
West Africa, right to the Atlantic. So we can see that the
African states of the Middle Ages had come into being practically when Egyptian-Sudanese antiquity came to its close.
The Nilotic Sudan was finally to lose its independence only in
the nineteenth century, and its old eastern province of
Ethiopia would retain its identity until the Italian occupation of 1936, barring which, it never lost its independence.
That being the case, Ethiopia is in point of fact the oldest
state in the world. Ghana lasted from about the third century AD until 1240, to be succeeded by Mali from that date to
1464 (accession of Soni-Ali, founder of the Songhay Empire).

The dismembering of these nations was effectively completed in the nineteenth century by the European occupation of Africa. The breaking-up went on apace; what we saw
then were tiny kingdoms, each jealous of its own independence, such as those of Cayor in Senegal conquered by
General Louis Faidherbe under Napoleon III after a fierce
resistance. The kingdoms of East Africa with trading cities
on the coast prospered from the end of classical antiquity
until the fifteenth and sixteenth centuries when they fell to
the Portuguese. These kingdoms maintained a lively trade
with India, Siam, and the Chinese Far East, evidenced both
by chronicles and by Chinese potteries found there. It is

hard for us today to picture the opulence of the authentically Black trading centers of that period. Father Gervase Mathew, of Oxford, in relating Swahili tradition mentions that in these cities there were silver staircases leading to beds of ivory. Such luxurious furnishing are barely imaginable today. The houses, built of stone, rose to five or six stories. The people were authentic jet-black Africans. Their women had shaven heads as in Ghana.

These civilizations were overthrown by the Portuguese who, in the sixteenth century, altered the old trade routes and sea lanes of the Indian Ocean. The conception of African history just briefly sketched is today to all intents and purposes accepted and endorsed by scholars:

> Black African culture set for the whole world an
> example of extraordinary vitality and vigor. All vi-
> talist conceptions, religious as well as philosophic, I
> am convinced, came from that source. The civiliza-
> tion of ancient Egypt would not have been possible
> without the great example of Black African culture,
> and in all likelihood it was nothing but the sublima-
> tion thereof.[1]

The history of the Nilotic Sudan, Egypt and present-day Ethiopia is well known. Until recently, however, the past of West Africa was related quite summarily. We have felt it necessary to bring this past to life through documents we have had at our disposal and by establishing a socio-historical analysis covering two thousand years.

The old political, social and economic organization of Black Africa over those two thousand years, the military, judicial, and administrative apparatus, the educational set-up, the university and technical levels, the pomp and circumstance of court life, the customs and mores—all details which had been presumed lost in the deep dark past—we were able to

bring strikingly and scientifically back to life, especially
insofar as West Africa was concerned, in *L'Afrique Noire
pré-coloniale* (Pre-Colonial Black Africa).[2]

A similar work should be undertaken for the Benin-Ifé
civilization. What would be of special interest there would be
the fact that even in its ideological superstructure the civilization of Benin borrowed nothing from either the Semitic or
the Aryan worlds. On the other hand, it does display a close
relationship with ancient Egypt, as might be expected: Its
art, in a certain measure, represents African sculptural
classicism.

The same kind of exhumation and revivification work on
our history for the period from antiquity to the present can
and must be undertaken in a systematic way for all of eastern, central, and southern Africa.

Egyptian, Greek, Roman, Persian, Chinese, and Arabic
documents known to exist and with what archeology may
add to them allow this to be done in large measure. Nowhere
in African history are there holes that cannot be filled in. The
empty spaces are only temporary, and the period that affects us runs without a break from Egyptian-Sudanese antiquity and fits right in sequence.

So, historical consciousness is properly restored. The
general framework of African history is set out. The evolution of peoples is known in its broad lines, but the research
already begun will have to be continued in order to fill the
small gaps that still exist, thus reinforcing the framework.
One can no longer see "darkest Africa" set against a "deep
dark past"; the African can clearly follow his evolution from
prehistory to our own day. Historical unity has become
manifest.

The psychological unity existing for all those who inhabit
the Dark Continent, and which each of us feels, is an elemen-
tary fact that needs no demonstration.

Geographical unity likewise is obvious, and it necessarily

implies economic unity. The latter is what we shall discuss in the pages devoted to the industrialization of Africa.

A consideration of the structure of the precolonial African family, that of the State, the accompanying philosophical and moral concepts, and the like, reveals a consistent cultural unity, resulting from similar adaptations to the same material and physical conditions of life. This was the subject of my *L'Unité culturelle de l'Afrique Noire* (The Cultural Unity of Black Africa).[3]

There is also a common linguistic background. The African languages constitute one linguistic family, as homogeneous as that of the Indo-European tongues. Nothing is easier than to set down the rules that allow transfer from a Zulu language (Bantu) to one of those of West Africa (Serer-Wolof, Peul), or even to ancient Egyptian (cf. *L'Afrique Noire pré-coloniale*, Part II). However, the old imperial languages, Sarakole in Ghana, Mandingo in Mali, Songhay in Koaga (Gao), have had their areas of extension sharply reduced today. At the apogee of these African empires, the imperial tongues, the languages of trade and government affairs, were the African languages themselves; even after the advent of Islam, Arabic always remained only the language of religion and erudition, as did Latin in Europe of the same period.

With European occupation in the nineteenth century the official African languages were replaced by those of the various "mother countries." Local dialects surfaced and vied against the older national cultural languages which had virtually submerged them. It became less and less necessary for civil administration, politics or social intercourse to learn the latter. The demands of daily life required learning the European languages; the disrepute of the old linguistic unities in our day reached its depth.

While we may be able to build a Federated African State covering all of the Black Continent on the basis of historical, psychological, economic and geographical unity, we will be forced, in order to complete such national unity and set it on a modern autochthonous cultural base, to recreate our linguistic unity through the choice of an appropriate African tongue promoted to the influence of a modern cultural language.

Linguistic unity dominates all national life. Without it, national cultural unity is but fragile and illusory. The wranglings within a bilingual country, such as Belgium, illustrate the point.

[1]Professor Georges Gurvitch, Sorbonne, "Message to the Second Convention of Black Writers and Artists," Rome, April, 1959 (in special issue, *Présence Africaine*).

[2]Paris: Éditions Présence Africaine, 1960. This work for the first time demonstrated the possibility of writing a history of Black Africa free of mere chronology of events. The type of study thus initiated, sometimes called "history of ideas," was immediately taken over by various historians, without benefit of acknowledgment, to be sure. (Cf. also, Diop, *The African Origin of Civilization*, cited above.)

[3]Paris: Éditions Présence Africaine, 1960.

Chapter Two
Linguistic Unity

1. Choice of Language on a Local Scale in the Framework of a Given Territory

Let us take Senegal as an example. Before any choice could be made, the kinship of the various tongues spoken in Senegal had to be demonstrated—which may not be as easily done in other territories. By setting out linguistic rules that would allow passage in a systematic way from Wolof forms to Serer, Peul-Toucouleur and Diola we demonstrated the deep kinship uniting the various segments of the Senegalese population.

The importance of this demonstration is that it shows us a kinship the ignorance of which had kept alive until the present local particularities (Serer, Diola or Toucouleur) at times as effectively uniting as mini-nations. Quite objectively, in a country such as Senegal, Wolof is the obvious choice for a national language, a language of government: All minorities are nearly bilingual, speaking Wolof in addition to their primary language. It can be seen that within the local context cultural languages, such as Peul-Toucouleur, fall into the class of minority groupings, whereas it is quite another matter in regions such as, say, Futa-Jallon or the Northern Cameroons.

2. Elevation of the Selected Language to the Level of a Modern Cultural and Government Language

It is in Wolof that researchers today are trying systematically to introduce all the concepts required to convey the exact sciences (mathematics, physics), philosophy and so on. An appropriate Senegalese government will one day apply a cultural policy aimed at favoring the development of the language in optimal order. It will be necessary to use artificial but effective methods, such as founding literary prizes, translating scientific works, creating a national commission to draw up an academic dictionary and various specialized ones (for mathematics, physics, philosophy, and so on).

Even now, we must start such work on a limited scale, in order to show once and for all that it is indeed possible to raise an African language to the prestige of any of the European cultural languages. What has so far been done and continues in this regard in Wolof has only exemplary value. Similar work must be judiciously carried out in the framework of each territory. The same criteria of selection will have to be applied in determining the territorial language with the same delicate study beforehand of linguistic, ethnic and other considerations in order to reduce any possibility of offending regional sensibilities.

As quickly as possible Wolof should become the language of government used in public and political documents and acts: parliamentary debate, drawing up of the constitution and legal code.

Until now, we have been in a period in which knowledge of the colonizing power's language was a prerequisite for holding any public office, especially that of deputy or legislator. Participating in debate in the French parliament made this indispensable. It is a paradox to continue such a state of affairs in any given African state. The major part of the population in any territory is still totally without knowledge of French; one can see that to elect people's representatives on outmoded criteria is patently inadequate and unjust. Using the colonizer's language is a convenient way to avoid facing the true complaints of the population, who may be illiterate but are not without good sense.

3. Choice of Language on a Continental Scale

When our demonstrations in Wolof have gone far enough, they will have proved that in due time it will be possible appropriately to choose one of the major African tongues and promote it to the level of sole governmental and cultural language for the entire continent. It will cover all territorial languages in the same way that Russian is overlaid on the language of each Socialist Republic within the Soviet Union.

The choice of such language will have to be made by a competent interterritorial commission imbued with deep patriotic feeling foreswearing any hidden chauvinism.

The language thus selected will at first be taught in the secondary schools of all territories, just as if it were an obligatory foreign language in the curriculum. Then, as textbooks on various subjects are completed in this language and adopted in high schools and colleges, the continental language will take the place of European languages as the vehicle for our modern national culture. European languages will not disappear from out schools but will progressively drop back to the position of elective foreign languages learned on a secondary-school level. A citizen of any given territory will be obliged to learn to speak fluently the continental language, while still being able to get secondary and even higher education in the territorial tongue.

Black writers and artists at their Rome convention (Easter, 1959) and the Federation of African Students in France at its July, 1959, seminar at Rennes, both officially adopted this view of the necessity and character of linguistic unity.[1]

During the transitional period, European languages will continue to be used, but that situation must not be allowed to endure too long, lest it eventually turn Africa into a super-Switzerland. There is nothing to be gained by urging simultaneous perpetuation of French, English, Portuguese, Spanish and Afrikaans, and why opt for exclusive use of either French or English?

We must remain circumspect about subtle efforts to
Anglo-Americanize Black Africa, considering how many of
the colonies were formerly British. The joint efforts of Great
Britain and of the United States especially run counter to
established "intellectual" habits and suggest to former
French, Portuguese, Spanish, or other colonies that they
ought to opt for English, so as to make that tongue the
lingua franca of the whole continent. Linguistic unity based
on a foreign language, however one may look at it, is cultural
abortion. It would irremediably eventuate in the death of
the authentic national culture, the end of our deeper intellectual and spiritual life and reduce us to perpetual copycats,
having missed out on our historical mission in this world.
Anglo-Saxon cultural, economic, social and even political
hegemony would thereby be permanently guaranteed
throughout Black Africa. We must remain radically opposed
to any attempts at cultural assimilation coming from the
outside: none is possible without opening the way to the
others.

One might say that it makes no difference to a Wolof-
speaking African whether he adopts Zulu or English or
Portuguese. This is just not so. An African educated in any
African language other than his own is less alienated, culturally speaking, than he is when educated in a European
language which takes the place of his mother tongue.
Likewise, a Frenchman who got an Italian education would
be much less alienated than if inculcated with Zulu or Arabic
in place of French. Such is the disparity in cultural interest
which exists between European and African languages—
something we must never lose sight of.

European languages must not be considered diamonds
displayed under a glass bell, dazzling us with their brilliance.
Our attention must rather be fixed on their historical development. Creatively, we discover that similar paths are open
to all.

The influence of language is so great that the various European mother countries feel they can afford to withdraw politically from Africa without great loss as long as their (linguistic) presence remains in the economic, spiritual and cultural spheres. They assume that onetime colonies will officially retain the colonizer's language; anything else would be disappointing, ungrateful and inacceptable. Such a design is impossible of realization, even though former colonies continue to honor the tongue of the mother country as the prime foreign language in high-school curricula. We are not at all talking of a radical cultural severance.

Because of the huge difficulties to be overcome in mastering the African linguistic mosaic, some observers in Europe are convinced that we will not be up to the challenge, that we will be unable to undertake a change requiring so much human energy, so much intellectual lucidity, so much creative thinking. If they do not actually sneer, they are nonetheless sure that the drive for African cultural unity will fail. Cultural surrender is a foregone conclusion, in view of the ignorance of vital problems that extends to some of our most responsible political leaders. Political independence to a certain degree is, yes, what they envision now. None of what makes for the greatness of modern nations in national culture or even economic infrastructure will, when all is said and done, ever exist among us, they assume. On the other hand, they firmly expect perpetuation of the cultural mix they create, and one can already hear the pseudo-dialectical phrases that will be used to try to legitimatize such a state of affairs in the name of efficiency, progress, planetary unity and what have you.[2]

Our generation is out of luck, so to speak, in what we will not be able to avoid the intellectual storm; willy-nilly, we will be forced to take the bull by the horns, to rid our minds of intellectual formulas and tidbits of thought in order to enter resolutely upon the only truly dialectical path toward the solution of the problems that history forces upon us. This connotes active research, in the most authentic meaning of that term, by clear and fertile minds capable of proposing effective solutions and realizing them without intellectual guardianship.

Historical circumstances now demand of our generation that it solve in a felicitous manner the vital problems that face Africa, most especially the cultural problem. If we do not succeed in this, we will appear in the history of the development of our people as the watershed generation that was unable to insure the unified cultural survival of the African continent; the generation which, out of political and intellectual blindness, committed the error fatal to our national future. We will have been the unworthy generation *par excellence.*

The selection of a single language for the continent—one which any foreigner, whether French, English, Russian, Indian, Chinese, Japanese, German, Dutch, Spanish, Portuguese, Italian or other, would have to learn to communicate with any African on our Black Continent—would thus obviously lead to a simplification of our intercourse with the outside world: International relations, far from becoming more complicated, would become much easier.

---

[1] As did the UNESCO-sponsored convention held at Bamako in 1964.

[2] I demonstrated (in *Nations nègres et culture,* Part II) the greater speed of assimilation of modern techniques through use of national languages and the multiple advantages of their systematic use as against use of European languages in educating the people.

Chapter Three
Political Unity and Federalism

The historical significance of national liberation movements in colonies, especially those of Black Africa, is no longer open to question. It is now readily admitted that this powerful decolonizing drive is as significant as the national movements of Europe during the nineteenth century. Apart from those colonies largely peopled by Europeans where resistance is inevitable, with few exceptions there is less and less violent opposition to the development of the movement. The new tactic rather consists in trying to direct it, channel it toward nonsocialistic forms, of the so-called Western type. If this goal were to be reached, the former colonial powers and the United States might stop worrying. Black Africa would be not Balkanized (for the political regimes of the Balkan countries are now relatively stable) but South-Americanized. It would be made up of a proliferation of little dictator-ridden countries without organic ties one to another, ephemeral, afflicted with chronic weakness, governed by terror with the help of outsized police forces, but under economic domination by foreign countries, pulling strings through the mere presence of an embassy. This was the case in Guatemala, where the following extraordinary situation occurred: A foreign business firm, the United Fruit Company (U.S.), overthrew the local government and replaced it with another more amenable to the company's aims, working in conjunction with the American embassy (and, as we now know, the CIA), thus proving the emptiness of the so-called independence of such a state.[1]

If we are to protect Black Africa from such a fate, the idea of federation must actually constitute—for all of us, especially those in high political positions—a method of survival (by way of an efficacious political and economic organization to be set up in optimum time), not just a dilatory demagogic formulation receiving merely lip service.

We must stop fooling the masses with minor patchwork and bring about the ultimate break with all the fake structures (*Communauté*, Commonwealth, Eurafrica) which have no historical future. Black Africa must finally and defnitively be started up the slope toward its federal destiny.

We cannot go on running with the hare and hunting with the hounds. The African countries, in the years ahead, will be forced progressively to strengthen their organic federal ties while ridding themselves of the remains of those that bind them still to their former "mother countries."

This need in no way result in economic chaos. West Africa alone, if federated, has an economic potential greater than that of France and England combined, that is, greater than that of the two countries most likely to impose economic sanctions on us. Naturally, that economic potential has to be developed. This creates problems of manpower and investment. In Part II of this program, we outline the path which can lead to the success of such an undertaking. Those in political power are the only ones who have not proved themselves up to coping with these problems, who indeed have never seriously given thought to them, who are terrified of taking the action which they conceive as economic weaning. They rather attempt, while acting as a screen, to perpetuate the same old economic/political guardianship in a more insidious manner, less visible to the masses but no less effective.

The proliferation of political leaders is a specifically African fact of life, resulting from colonization by different imperial powers and the consequent breaking up into administrative territories of conquered regions. It constitutes a serious difficulty that will have to be taken into account in any attempts at African continental unification.

No concrete way has yet been proposed that might lead inevitably and rapidly to a federation of African States, with partial or total surrender of local sovereignty. For all the fine public statements, multifarious individual and general interests are at work to make people cling to the established frontiers of the various territories.

No one has even suggested any sort of cartel of presidents or heads of state as an embryo federal government, which might be broadened gradually as the various states become emancipated. This might be the way to provide a collective directorship within which no one chief of state would hold the top position, pending full independence of the continent. Individual states' interests could thus be safeguarded at the same time as African unity.

On the other hand, the establishment of some kind of consultative assembly, the organization of a Latin American-type debating society, can in the long run lead only to an increasingly tolerated and finally fully accepted ossification of the various frontiers of African States. This would unavoidably mean a mosaic as in South America.[2]

Continental States

Unification of the entire planet does not seem likely in the immediate future, whatever a superficial mind might think of it. The social consciousness of the world, at this juncture, is far from having been sufficiently awakened for certain half-hidden feelings to be extirpated from it. Eternal vigilance remains an urgent prerequisite to eventual world unity.

What are sometimes called "grand designs" do not readily fit in with the history and interests of peoples. When the true faults within them become apparent, they will doubtless follow the shape of continents for a period now difficult to assess. Nor will that period under any circumstances be shortened by anything but mutual respect or fear of one another's powers. Sincere fraternization and the unity of the planet will be possible only when the various peoples are equal in strength, and advanced to the point where none can any longer hope to deceive any of the others. The formation of continental states would appear to be a preliminary step toward planetary unity.

This is the more likely since Europe which, by itself, colonized nearly all of the globe, might well take umbrage when it reaches the end of its delusions and clearly understands it has lost all of its former colonies. European unification in that case might be based on bitterness, as suggested by certain flareups of neo-Nazism (Christmas, 1959) perhaps less devoid of deeper significance than some have alleged. Europe might well turn in upon itself and adopt a neonationalism encompassing all of Western Europe.[3]

Hunger in the Year 2000

A short-sighted political leader might today drive his country toward catastrophe. Despite all the improvements in living conditions that can be anticipated from the amazing accomplishments of science, some problems—such as feeding the earth's uncontrollably growing population—will not be solved in the near future. Scientists are already wondering how we will feed the six billion inhabitants of the globe in the year 2000—less than a quarter-century from now. This is of such urgency that a branch of the United Nations, the Food and Agricultural Organization (FAO), was given the job of studying world hunger. All it came up with is the suggestion that the underdeveloped countries be fed on fish meal. Other scientists have been urging the cultivation of algae. Some influential American groups have even recommended to their government that its foreign economic aid be restricted to those underdeveloped nations which agree to limit their birthrates. This is an obvious Malthusian approach.

Repopulation of Africa

It is clear that a continent such as Black Africa, the sole victim of slavery in modern times (with 100 to 200 million people killed or carried away), can only turn a deaf ear on any such suggestions. Our continent, with its demographic emptiness, has an imperative duty to apply a systematic policy of intensive repopulation in optimum time. Black Africa contains sufficient sources of natural energy, raw materials, and foodstuffs to feed and sustain such a population. It must avoid in the future becoming the receptacle for the rest of the world's human overflow. It cannot consider large-scale immigration from abroad, even for its least-populated regions (such as Central Africa), until it has regained a strong national personality capable of assimilating the outlander instead of vice versa.

All the hypocritical decisions that might be conceived along these lines on an international level by any organization, however apparently prestigious, must be rejected out of hand by us. Along these lines, the 1960 conference held at Tangier by a UN commission, presided over by the late Dag Hammarskjold, was a straw in the wind. The then Secretary General forthrightly expressed the opinion that the appearance of Africa on the world political scene would within the year create a problem concerning representation of two different categories of countries, dramatically differing not only in their levels of capabilities but even more so in their numbers: the technically developed and the underdeveloped nations. This suggested that a reorganization of the statutes might be considered, so that the influence of older "civilized" European countries would not be outweighed by the mass of newcomers. This would mean nothing less than a directorate, already advocated by some heads of states.[4] But how could this result in anything other than the failure of the entire organization?

The Yellow Peril

The West's frenzied haste to undertake disarmament reflects a latent malaise, a hidden fear, which had seemed to be gone forever: that of the Yellow Peril. The more or less skillfully conducted debates have shown that the aim has been to bring France into line (on the question of atomic capability) so as to set a moral precedent that might be used, when needed, to condemn China to perpetual military inferiority by keeping her out of the atomic club. The interests of the capitalist world as a whole would have, of course, dictated that France give up becoming an atomic power. Not only would she thus have shown her willingness to stay in line, but also the higher interests of the Western camp would have been safeguarded to the extent that, having already its own atomic weapons, it could use a moral argument to dissuade China from developing any. The latter country is, after all, a yellow or colored power.

In certain circles one often hears expressions of concern at seeing such a power appear and fear of what it might become by the year 2000—with a full arsenal of atomic weapons. There is talk of China overflowing, of it swallowing up Europe in a full-scale replay of Attila the Hun. Efforts are made (by various means which may well have a broader scope at a later date), artificially to keep this absurd fear alive in nonsocialist minds and consciences, the idea being to stimulate a panic causing reflexive reactions in self-defense. What is especially feared is rapprochement between Asia and Africa.

The fact that France failed to hear the call, and that the moral/political maneuver directed against China did not work out, merely proves—if proof still be needed—that the capitalist world is full of insurmountable contradictions. Many Western politicos and military men welcome the split that has occurred between the Soviet Union and the People's Republic of China, which is interpreted as the same kind of self-defense reflex on the part of the USSR, a "white nation having conquered part of Asia." They hope to see the rift maintained, despite any socialist objectives and interests those two powers might share.

Frontiers

How far would the Federated African State extend? Roughly speaking, from the Tropic of Cancer to the Cape, from the Indian Ocean to the Atlantic.

In *L'Afrique Noire pré-coloniale*, we showed what had been the historical frontiers of those old West African Black empires. They virtually followed the Tropic of Cancer. The border province of Teghezza is on that parallel. We know the name of one of the last Black governors there representing the Askia of Kaoga (Gao): the Teghezza-Mondzo, Mohammed Ikoma.

The Saharan zone that separates the Tropic of Cancer from the latitude of Sidjilmessa has never known constituted authority. It was the appanage of the Messouffa Berbers, who for a fee served as guides to caravans going through the corridors of the desert which they had explored.

I think there was great merit in the idea put forth by the

late Moroccan progressive Mehdi Ben Barka, when he said
that all questions of frontiers today are made inoperative by
the general evolution of Africa as a whole.

[1]Since these lines were first written, this process of South-Americanization has indeed begun
in Black Africa. The phenomenon has become generalized: civilian governments are today the
exception.

[2]The existence of the Organization of African Unity since 1963 has largely confirmed this view.
(Translator's Note)

[3]More recently, neo-Nazism has indeed reappeared in West Germany and in some countries of
Latin America (Chile, Brazil, and Argentina among them).

[4]The very existence of the Security Council perpetuates "weighted votes" (that is, proportional
to the strength of the great powers).

Chapter Four
The Privileged Position of West Africa

After the failure of the Europeans' attempts to coordinate their colonial policies, West Africa became the arena in which France and England strove to outbid each other politically. Great Britain, having established no heavily settled colonies there, could easily create difficulties for France since all of France's African colonies, unlike those of the British Empire, were concentrated in West and Equatorial Africa.

As long as the discovery of Algeria's immense wealth of resources did not change France's colonial outlook, she found it hard to adjust to the British, who were withdrawing from West Africa the better to consolidate their East African settlement colonies (Kenya, Tanganyika, the Rhodesias, even South Africa, which to a certain extent falls into the same category). The lessons of the wars in Indochina and North Africa as well as the discovery of resources of the Sahara made it easier for the French to face up to the competitive situation. The destinies reserved for political movements in West and East Africa were to be quite different. One need only compare the fierce repression of the Mau-Maus with the negotiated recognition of independence for British West Africa (Nigeria, for example) or French West Africa. This accounts for the relative ease with which West African political problems (with the exception of those in the Cameroons) were solved by negotiation rather than gunfire. That ease did not, however, permit political cleansing nor reinforcement of national consciousness. What can be called the privileged position of West Africa may entail lasting consequences. Virtually all of Africa, with the exception of Rhodesia, Namibia, and South Africa, now is free.

This difference in treatment is due to the presence of white minorities in the various territories of the East and South. The struggle that had to be carried on in these regions was very much akin to what had gone on in North Africa and to the struggle which we will all in the last analysis have to join in together in South Africa. The real powderkeg of the Black Continent remains in the South.

White States

There can be no compromise, and we will in the future allow no creation of White states in whatever form or for whatever pretext, regardless of the apparent prestige of the hypocritical international organization proposing such states. We will drive no one out, for we are not racists. We will wipe out no minority but will insist upon democratically proportional participation in the way states are governed. We will not accept stratification of national life in these future states on an ethnic basis. No country, until now, has solved its minority problem in any other manner.

Those who cannot serve us as examples, are not qualified to offer us advice, much less give us orders.

Historical Mission of West and Equatorial Africa

The historical mission of West Africa to a large extent consists in taking advantage of the facilities history has given it to lose no time in becoming a powerful federated state, capable of freeing the rest of the continent by force if need be, rather than continuing indefinitely in weakness, divisiveness and with the declamatory promises of oppor-

tunistic patriots. We can already sense the political consequences mentioned above. There has been no political work
accomplished that might radically have transformed consciences or prepared them for the austere tasks required by
true independence.

National problems are still being met with a bureaucratic
mentality. This accounts for the lack of any cultural policies
worthy of the name in the first independent West African
nations. None has adopted a systematic policy of restoration
of the national language, and the only ones to adopt African
languages as their official tongues have been Tanzania and
then Kenya with Swahili. (UNESCO, taking over the ideas
in the second part of our *Nations nègres et culture* about the
development of African national languages, did establish a
program of support for African states toward this end and in
1970 held a seminar on national languages in Tanzania.)

None has attempted without delay to set up a powerful
modern army with a properly equipped air force, civilian-
trained, unsuited to the putsches common in Latin America
and capable of measuring up on short notice to historical
tasks we might find facing us. On the contrary, we risk
having nothing more than embryo armies with outmoded
equipment, no air force, no ballistic missiles, yet counterbal-
anced by ultramodern dictatorial police forces.

Nothing will do but that we make up for the relative ease
of our liberation through an immense effort of political education and cultural formation. Otherwise we may find ourselves opposing foreign nationalisms that are still expansive
and inured to armed struggle with a mere folkloric nation-
alism endowed only with the piebald local colors of our native
woven fabrics.

Nothing indeed could be more amazing, more fantastic,
than the sight of the French head of state in Paris on the
Place de la Concorde on Bastille Day of 1959, giving out
colorful little national flags to the heads of state of the
Communauté countries!

What can "retaining control of an independent country" mean?

If we are willing to go along with this capitalist process of bourgeoisification—which can only be fatal to the political health of our country—if we agree to becoming this auxiliary class of international high finance, fine and dandy. If, even better, we proclaim, "We are your spiritual and intellectual sons, your Black incarnation; just make us recipients of your financial and moral interests in due time, and the situation will be saved! One will no longer see you, although you will still be here. We will act as a screen; it will not longer be you, but we, Africans, who will defend your ideals against other Africans"—if we say all that, it will be grand!

That is why (and how) this new "liberal" policy—in order to be entirely effective and not too idealistic—has been everywhere (except in Guinea, where there was not time for it) underpinned with the setting-up of right-thinking politicos, with a whole supporting infrastructure. This new "liberal" policy has everywhere resulted in the eviction of true revolutionary movements and the triumph of traditionally conformist groupings. It tends everywhere to pass off these same conformists, in the eyes of the people, as pseudo-revolutionaries, so as to give them credence. The situation in Cameroon (1959–1960) in this regard was typical. One really wonders, assuming independence were purely and simply granted, what would keep France from remaining neutral toward the various parties and accepting in advance authentic elections if that were the only way to bring to power a team of leaders of the people's choice, assure general tranquility and stabilize the political situation.

But there are powerful material interests at work (Edea Dam, bauxite refinery). It would be unthinkable to favor a revolutionary team that might once again call so many interests into question. Something must be done, then, to keep the people of the Cameroon from thinking they owe their independence to Um Nyobé's party. We are already everywhere and very severely undergoing the calculated inconveniences of internal autonomy, which is said to be the preparatory stage for independence: the division of revolutionary forces (before full and meaningful independence) in a manner that will make it difficult to recoalesce everywhere with equal ease; the ever-more solid stratification of African society into classes in the modern economic sense of the term; the virtual impossibility, as a result, of avoiding a class struggle in Black Africa.

Slogans do not engage the minds and hearts of the working masses and even less those of bureaucrats—for "Stakhanovism" and economic austerity can have meaning only within the framework of true independence, none at all within a regime conceived to improve foreign capitalistic production in full safety, using expedients which not all of the people can fail to perceive. Grandiose perspectives on the building of a strong modern continent-wide African state would permit creation of enthusiasm, a sense of abnegation and true patriotic feeling. Then—and only then—would the problem of national independence cease to be expressed in terms of wages (as is the case with those who are already muttering, "We would have been better off leaving things the way they were"). All of the foregoing expresses the absence of any revolutionary parties in power, anywhere in the *Communauté*.

Along the same lines, in order to counter the budding anti-intellectualism evident throughout Black Africa among those in political power, as if this were a defense mechanism, intellectuals have to be able to present perspectives for Africa, solutions to problems on a national scale which allow of no other possible ways out. The intellectuals must gain respect at the same time through their efficiency, their taste for unselfish work on behalf of the people, and their clarity.

They must be sincere, and to do that they must truly feel themselves animated by an ideal that will stand come what may. They must set themselves apart from those minds which shine only with deceptive light, as artificial as it is sterile, the flashy pseudo-intelligences that so readily prove to be insignificant.

Self-defense anti-intellectualism would spell a new loss of Africa if it were to become general. We cannot afford the luxury of rejecting what we have most been missing during these last three centuries.

[1]Algeria gained independence on July 3, 1962, and maintains full diplomatic relations with France. *(Translator's Note)*

Chapter Five

The New Strategy

General de Gaulle acted like a true strategist toward the colonies, hoping to kill any spirit of struggle or opposition to the mother country by depriving that opposition of visible reason.

He is reported to have said, "Territories which for ten years have not ceased dreaming of independence today are insistently demanding it. Should we allow this movement to grow against us or on the contrary attempt to understand, assimilate and channel it properly?"

This idea had grown out of a long meditation (dating back to the Fourth Republic immediately following World War II) on the possibility of maintaining colonialism.

The Indochinese and North African experiences served to forestall events in Black Africa. They allowed the granting of independence which was otherwise going to be seized. "I loosened the bonds before they were sundered," DeGaulle is reported to have said.

This was an act of high strategy obviously intended to atrophy our national consciousness, to reduce it and render it assimilable to all sorts of mixes. If he could win this "wager," the historical destiny of the continent might be checked. But all wagers of this kind, defying the destinies of peoples, have historically been lost. Otherwise, Eurafrica, with its "horizontal" and "vertical" links, would have come into being in an even more insidious and flexible form. The confederation now a-borning would then have been only another aspect of it, more suitably adapted to the circumstances. Toward that end, a convention was organized on the Riviera in November, 1959, bringing together African polit-

ical leaders and European industrialists, among whom the
presence of many Germans was notable. All the magnates of
European industry who envisaged transforming Africa into
a politically stabilized field for economic expansion were
there, eagerly seeking valuable interlocutors. They had to
have political guarantees before they would hazard any investment.

Since the end of World War II, it had become evident that
for such a condition to endure it was necessary to create a
true native industrial, financial, and banking bourgeoisie,
whose class interests would thenceforth coincide with those
of international high finance. But this had been all too slow in
coming about . . . It was a mistake of the European
bourgeoisies that they were now trying to remedy within
the time limits history allowed. Then the Saharan oilfields
were discovered, and the French colonial outlook was totally
transformed.

The French bourgeoisie thinks it will be, henceforth, most
practical to tie in with Algeria. They think this can be
done—at least more readily than they could bring off the old
French Union or even the now-secondary *Communauté*.
France is ready to admit that sooner or later Black Africa
will be lost, in view of the modest military pressure that can
be brought to bear and the irreversible evolutionary cycle
which the Dark Continent has entered; before the inevitable, best to bow with good grace.

On the other hand, France believes that the presence of a
minority in North Africa and proximity of the territory (as
against France's distance from Indochina) are factors
militating in favor of the maintenance of its authority there.
By concentrating its efforts on Algeria, France has hoped to
have a permanent source of energy and varied ores that she
had previously been in the habit of seeking much farther
afield (and outside the zone of her own currency). She be-

lieves she can become virtually the premier power in Western Europe, where energy is concerned.

Henceforth, in a parallel movement, she is becoming more liberal toward Black Africa, so as to reconquer on an emotional level the friendship of the former, perhaps embittered colonies while trying to grind up and assimilate Algeria.[1]

We are still not free, however, even after this loosening of bonds. We will never be allowed to select a political and social regime different from those of the Western World without running the risk of having to fight or seeing ourselves overthrown by intrigues, making use of local parties of Western allegiance. This is the last camouflaged line of retreat for the batteries of the imperialist West, alleging that its own economic fate and "civilization as we know it" depend on retaining control of Africa.

Chapter Six
Bicameralism

A study of our past can give us a lesson in government. Thanks to the matriarchal system, our ancestors prior to any foreign influence had given woman a choice place. They saw her not as sex object but as mother. This has been true from the Egypt of the Pharaohs until our time.[1] Women participated in running public affairs within the framework of a feminine assembly, sitting separately but having the same prerogatives as the male assembly.[2]

These facts remained unchanged until the colonial conquest, especially is such non-Islamized States as the Yoruban and Dahomean. Behanzin's military resistance to the French Army under Colonel Dodds is said to have resulted from a decision of the women's assembly of the kingdom, meeting at night after the men had met during the day and reversing them by ordering mobilization and war—after which, the men ratified the decision.

Black Africa had its specific bicameralism, determined by sex. Far from interfering with national life by pitting men against women, it guaranteed the free flowering of both. It is to the honor of our ancestors that they were able to develop such a type of democracy. Wherever we find this as late as the Aegean period, the southern Black influence is undeniable. In reestablishing it in modern form, we remain faithful to the democratic and profoundly human past of our forebears; once and for all, we relax the society of mankind by freeing it from a latent millennial contradiction. We might without any doubt inspire other countries in ordering their affairs.

To reestablish this ancestral bicameralism on a modern basis means we must find along with our women and to the exclusion of any type of demagoguery a truly efficacious mode of representation for the feminine element of the nation. The setting-up of this assembly, the method of electing its members and the structure of the basic building blocks of the militant parties of Black Africa are, therefore, so many practical problems to be solved.

Such reforms would allow the normalization of the political role of woman, the restoration of her dignity as the mother of the family, the realization once and for all in an efficient meaningful manner of what every country calls women's rights.

A comparable experiment was carried out in the USSR under Stalin at the beginning of Socialist construction but only in the domain of production. The women's assemblies created were to assume an educational role and especially production duties. Everywhere, the results were prodigious; the assemblies were dissolved before World War II when Socialist construction was sufficiently developed so there was no longer need to distinguish between womanpower and manpower. Such assemblies existed after 1945 in the newer federated republics of the Soviet Union, where social development was not so advanced, such as the Ukraine, Byelo-Russia, Latvia, and they are still operating.

Some of my compatriots feel that for the present we should be satisfied with simply a consultative assembly for women.

NOTE: I am especially indebted to Professor Diop Issa for helping me in reworking and adapting this chapter.

[1]Cf. Matriarchy, *The African Origin of Civilization: Myth or Reality*, pp. 142–145.

[2]In Senegal, in certain cases one refers to a man who governs according to custom as *N' Deye Dj Rèv* (Mother of the Country), and no one is shocked by it. This customary reference still exists among the Lebous.

Part II
Compendium of Energy Sources

Hydraulic Energy

World reserves of hydraulic energy are estimated at 50 billion kilowatt-hours per year, of which almost 90 percent are concentrated in underdeveloped regions; Europe has only 3 percent, the United States 4 percent, and the USSR 3.5 percent.

At the present rate of development, France will have exhausted its hydraulic potential in less than a decade. Harnessing the few remaining waterfalls in France or the U.S. would be prohibitively costly in view of their locations.

Black Africa leads all the world in hydraulic energy with its reserves of thousands of billions of kilowatt-hours representing about half the total world resources. The Zaire River, second largest in volume of flow (30,000 to 60,000 cubic meters per second) by itself holds more than 600 billion kilowatt-hours of annual reserves or two-thirds of the entire production of the world at the present time, the Sanaga and Ogooué half as much. Engineers have calculated that the Sanaga (Cameroon), having its source at 1400 meters altitude and a flow three times that of the Rhône at the Génissiat hydroelectric plant, could deliver as much energy as all of the waterways of the French Alps combined.

Black Africa, through its hydraulic resources alone, is one of the world leaders in energy. Hydraulic energy is not comparable to uranium ore which, if need be, can be exported. Up to the present, hydraulic power has had to be used on the spot, and with alternating current can be delivered only over relatively insignificant distances, but Soviet and Swedish technicians have recently accomplished great advances in the long-haul delivery of electric power.

When electrical energy is transmitted by alternating current, line reactance, comparable to enormous resistance, accounts for tremendous losses en route so that huge though the originating voltage may be (400,000 volts) it finally delivers only very slight energy if the distance is of any magnitude. If instead of alternating we could use direct current, line reactance would disappear. What Soviet and Swedish engineers have done is to maintain alternating current at the source with generators that produce several tens of thousands of volts. Transformers then raise the tension to a threshold of a million volts, reversing the current and making it ready for transmission in direct current. Jean Rivoire has shown that Sweden is beyond the theoretical stage in this matter: Since February, 1954, an underwater cable has been carrying energy from Sweden to the island of Gotland at 200,000 direct-current volts, and it could carry as much as 600,000 volts. If a million volts were reached at an intensity of a thousand amperes, each line of this type would transmit a million kilowatts, and its full capacity in one year would be nine billion kilowatt-hours.

Once the problem of moving electrical energy in the form of direct tension has been solved, harnessing the hydroelectric power of the Zaire Basin alone (Inga and Kisangani dams) could supply all of the Black Continent with electricity.

Solar Energy

On an average the sun daily sends to earth 10^{15} kWh (one quadrillion kilowatt-hours), that is to say, a quantity of energy comparable to the sum total of all the energy resources in oil, coal, uranium and natural gas at present known to exist on our planet. Each square kilometer on which the sun shines each day gets a quantity of energy equivalent to that of an ordinary atomic bomb. However

topical atomic energy may be, scientists agree that solar
energy is that of the future, since it will exist as long as there
is sun. Hydraulic energy, having a comparable permanence,
is indirectly dependent on it to the extent that the sun affects
our weather. From Archimedes to Félix Trombes, men have
tried to tame the sun, and today they are near the point of
success.

Solar energy can be utilized in a direct form. To do this,
one must (as Félix Trombes did at Mont-Louis in the
Pyrenees) cover a parabolic surface with small rectangular
mirrors in adjustable positions. Depending on the surfaces
involved, the focus of the great parabolic mirror thus
created could reach a temperature as high as 3000°C
(5400°F), the heat of the solar atmosphere itself. Félix
Trombes has succeeded in using solar forces to melt metallic
oxides which heretofore had been completely refractory. A
solar oven uses solar heat directly: at Mont-Louis, a metric
half-ton of iron can be melted in a day. An even more gigantic
project was planned in the north Sahara at Colombéchard
under the direction of the same scientist. It was to deliver
1000 kilowatts of power but was abandoned as a result of the
war in Algeria.

If instead of trying to achieve a high temperature concentrated at one spot in an oven the dimension and shape of the
mirror were varied to spread the heat over an axis, enough
steam could be accumulated to operate a power plant. The
heated axis could then be girt by tubing filled with oil, which
would be extended into a boiler of water to which it would
transmit its calories. This is the Schumann method that was
used at Maadi, Egypt (in a purely experimental plant, no
longer operating).

In the most efficient solar connectors, the direction of the
mirrors is synchronized to the movement of the sun. Such
installations are limited by the enormousness of their size,
the state of the sky and, therefore, the latitude and the

alternation of day and night. Nothing daunted, some scientists, hoping for plants that can run without shutting down at night, are studying the operation of chlorophyll in greenery to determine how solar energy is stored in leaves.

There is a solar plant in operation at Tashkent, USSR, that produces electric power.

Solar energy can be utilized in an indirect form by employing solar cells made of semiconductors (silicon, germanium, etc.). These techniques have become common and require no further elaboration here. Home electrical energy can now be supplied directly by the sun and soon solar panels will be mass-produced. Man is no longer slave to oversized machinery. Calculators are common and can slip into a breast pocket when once they were larger than chests of drawers.

Due to the cost of silicon surfaces, solar energy does not appear to be any cheaper than hydroelectric power at present, but it remains a prime future energy source. Present expectations are that future installations will not be on the equator itself, because of the permanent cloud cover there, but territories on either side of the tropics might be ideal for solar installations: Sahara, Libya, all of the Sudanese zone as far as Ethiopia and a large part of the southern African region.

Atomic Energy

Controlled fission of uranium and thorium is at the basis of atomic energy. A chain reaction is created, giving off enormous heat. Two thousand metric tons of uranium 235 are the energy equivalent of all the world's reserves of petroleum.

Current concern with atomic energy makes a discussion of its properties unnecessary here. We can say that it will become part of the industrial equipment of all modern nations within the next ten years or so. Until 1952, the then Belgian Congo supplied 50 percent of the world's production of uranium. Today, Africa in all likelihood comes immediately after Canada and the United States with its nearly five thousand metric tons of uranium metal in marketable concentrations (Zaire and South Africa combined).[1]

There is uranium in Ethiopia, Cameroon, Nigeria, the Sahara, Zaire, Ghana, Zambia, Mozambique, Uganda and the Union of South Africa, where a thorium mine has also been found at the Cape. A good deal of vigilance must be exercised in the exploitation of nuclear energy. The material supplying the energy (uranium and thorium) is not comparable to hydroelectric or solar power, which one would be hard put to carry away in bottles. It is a simple ore, and Africa might easily be stripped of it in record time while it was being stored elsewhere—if the political future were to become uncertain while mechanized mining was allowed without limit.

Breeders, using high-velocity sodium-cooled neutrons, are the reactors of the future for the industrial exploitation of atomic energy. It has been calculated that when present research is perfected these reactors will produce more fuel (plutonium) than they consume—which seems something of a miracle. It is in this form, and other kindred ones, that Black Africa will have to consider the matter of its industrial nuclear outfitting.

Thermonuclear Energy

Atomic, or more properly nuclear, energy is a first step in the creation of thermonuclear energy. A mass of uranium, disintegrating within a confine containing a certain variety of hydrogen (deuterium or tritium) in a millionth of a second creates heat on the scale of 16 million degrees Centigrade (or 29 million degrees Fahrenheit) comparable to that inside the hot stars, especially the sun (26,000,000°C, 36,000,000°F). This little sun with its temperature is indispensable to overcome Coulombian resistance, to bring about the fusion of two hydrogen nuclei and produce helium with a slight loss of mass. This lost mass takes the form of radiating calorific energy: In order to evaluate it, one must multiply the mass by the square of the speed of light, that is 9×10^{10}, according to Einstein's formula. The enormous heat of the fusion of hydrogen nuclei due to the reduction of mass adds to the heat of the atomic fission of the uranium, explaining why the H-bomb frees so much more energy than the A-bomb. Unlike atomic energy, thermonuclear energy is not yet available for industrial use.

In a reactor, or atomic pile, a chain reaction can be started; it can be intensified, then held to a given temperature as long as desired and afterwards turned off by pushing in or pulling out the boron or cadmium steel bars that regulate the flow of neutrons—the neutrons being the bombardment agents that start the chain reaction (the degree of reaction or intensity depends on their flow). As this is written, thermonuclear reactors are still largely the province of theoreticians.

The British team headed by John Cockcroft, which thought it had discovered how to create controlled fusion without the use of an atomic starter, has been proven wrong. The neutrons, the presence of which was supposed to have been the team's proof, turned out to have come from the outside, perhaps from the walls of the casing or a fission of deuteron nuclei as a result of the weakness of the neutron-proton combination (2.2 Mev as against 30 Mev for helium as a result of the saturation of nuclear forces). The process used was probably the same found by a young Russian researcher. A reactor is a huge ring, the center axis of whicn is a column of combustible gas (deuteron) to be fused without coming in contact with the walls. An external coil creates the large magnetic field required to keep the column of gas away from the walls. Indeed, whatever the walls were made of, they would melt at the temperature of 4 to 16 million degrees Centigrade, which the column of gas should reach through powerful electrical discharges. This method holds some hope for the control of thermonuclear energy. No one at present is able to put forward a date at which thermonuclear energy will be controlled on an industrial basis. There might be a sudden leap ahead that would allow quick perfecting of a fusion method, but there could just as well be a very long wait for that. The continuing interest shown by industrial powers in the classic source of energy, oil, tells us that we are still far from thermonuclear substitutes which may eventually take the place of all others.[2]

Once thermonuclear reaction has become adapted to industry mankind will without doubt, as the scientists foresee, have an abundant new source of energy. Electrolysis of sea water would become a direct source of the indispensable raw material, heavy hydrogen or deuteron present in sea water to the extent of .02 percent. This tiny percentage is not be be scoffed at, considering the enormous temperature reached by fusion.

Production and processing centers would necessarily have to be near the sea in Africa. A territory such as Zaire would be in especially good position. Indeed, in view of what was said above, creation of thermonuclear energy will first require expenditure of an enormous amount of electrical energy for electrolysis. Hydraulically created electricity could prove economical for such an operation. The fact remains that at present we must go by way of atomic energy to get to thermonuclear energy, and until new discoveries have been made, the quantity of hydrogen for fusion will depend on the amount of fissionable material the earth disgorges.

These are the great energy sources within Black Africa

which, in and of themselves, could make this continent one of the most highly industrialized. Although the future of energy research is full of promise, we have listed here only those energy sources that exist in quantity today. This is why we have not discussed either oil or coal. The future place of these two sources in the African economy is undeniable. Pessimism of bygone years has given way to the greatest hopes, based on tangible indices. An enlightened policy will consist of encouraging further exploration and development in the double area of coal and oil, in which Black Africa is not now self-sufficient.[3]

One must also take note of other complementary energy sources mentioned by some authors, such as Ivan du Jonchay, as due to become important in the future.

Wind Energy

It has been discovered that, thanks to the tradewinds, the entire West Coast of Africa could be equipped with huge windmills, as could the Cape region. The Canaries and Kerguelens are already so equipped. It would be wrong to minimize this source of energy, since in Denmark, for instance, wind energy supplies 15 percent of national requirements. Wind-motors or windmills would do wonderfully for initially irrigating the soil and supplying water to cattle in the impoverished semiarid regions of Senegal, such as the Ferlo, Cayor, part of Baol and Djambour.

Thermal Energy of the Seas

Carnot's formula can be used to power a plant through the temperature differential at the sea's bottom and its surface. The method employed is that of Georges-Claude Boucherot.

It was applied at Abidjan between the coastal lagoon and a ditch known as a "bottomless pit," five hundred meters deep. The temperature differential is 22 degrees Centigrade (70 degrees Fahrenheit), enough to make a 7500-kilowatt powerhouse practicable, according to du Jonchay *(op. cit.).*

The Djander region in Senegal is equally well suited to installation of this type of plant. However, one drawback which has been insufficiently anticipated is delaying the work. By creating a vacuum, it is possible to make water within an enclosure boil at 70 degrees Fahrenheit and give off steam that can be directed at turbines to produce electricity. The gases contained in salt water are simultaneously released in the vacuum and create a bubbling that impedes the operation. What is required is advance degasification of an enormous mass of several tons of water within a closed circuit if boiling in the vacuum at low temperature is to be successfully achieved, giving off homogeneous steam to drive the turbines of the powerhouse. This may be one of the reasons for the Abidjan project having been discontinued.

Tidal Energy

Making use of the movements of the tides, one can harness an appropriate estuary and create reservoirs, some of which, being relatively high up, might be filled by siphoning at high tide. The reservoirs thus created would act exactly as do the holding lakes behind dams. At low tide, the water would flow from these reservoirs toward the turbines to keep them working.

The drawbacks of tidal energy are twofold: installation

and equipment are so costly as to be affordable only by a great economic power. The sites that prove practical, after detailed studies of terrain, are rare. The difference between high and low tide has to be very impressive, in the neighborhood of eight meters (almost twenty-seven feet). In France, the Bay of Mont-St.-Michel and the estuary of the Rance would be suited for such huge enterprises, but actual undertaking of the projects, which would result in economic rebirth for all surrounding areas, is continually postponed because of the enormous costs involved. The French National Electrical Company has calculated that by creating such a powerhouse it would be able to supply fully half of France's present energy needs (25 to 30 billion kilowatt-hours per annum).

It would be of interest to survey the rise of sea tides in the estuaries of African rivers, especially those of the Senegal River, the effect of which can be felt as far upstream as Podor, and the Salum, Gambia, and Casamance rivers. The theory of tidal-energy powerhouses is fairly complex; it even includes the earth's rotation within its margins for error. We will return to this question in discussing the industrialization of Mali (former Senegal-Sudan Federation).

Global Heat

Carnot's principle can be applied, too, to the temperature differential between the earth's surface and a hot subterranean source reached by drilling. This differential could boil water and produce steam under a vacuum at well below 100° Centigrade (212° Fahrenheit). Research and a start toward application have already been carried out in Zaire (du Jonchay, *op. cit.*).

Volcanic Thermal Energy and Geothermal Energy

This can be employed on the spot by thermal generators that send into pipes buried in lava a great mass of water which, as it evaporates, delivers steam to be directed to operating turbines. The circuit is a closed one, and the recondensed vapor after being used is returned by a pumping system back into the lava. This might be installed at the foot of Mount Cameroon in Kenya. Generally speaking, all of East Africa (Ethiopia, Kenya, Uganda, Tanzania and the entire Rift Valley region) would be eminently suited for the installation of plants powered by geothermal energy.

These are the energy resources of Black Africa. Their utilization by Africans themselves—not to create industries to supplement those of Europe but to process the raw materials that the continent contains—could turn Black Africa into a paradise on earth.[4]

[1]These were 1959–1960 figures. More recent figures reveal the following:

Current Uranium Resources (1975)		Production
Black Africa (including South Africa)	272,800 metric tons	4736 metric tons
United States	262,000 metric tons	8840 metric tons
Canada	185,000 metric tons	3560 metric tons

[2]What was ture of thermonuclear development in 1959 is still largely true today. However, the use of lasers to incite thermonuclear reactions does allow for great hopes. JET (the Joint European Torus), which makes use of the "Tokomak configuration" developed by Soviet researchers, is planned to demonstrate the possibility of controlling thermonuclear reaction on a practical level. If it proves successful, it will be time to go on to the next stage, the construction of the first prototype thermonuclear reactors, which should probably occur in the year 2000.

[3]Since this was first written, oil deposits have been discovered in Gabon, Nigeria, Senegal, Angola and the Congo. Cf. Ivan du Jonchay, *Industrialisation de l'Afrique* (The Industrialization of Africa) (Paris: Payot, 1953).

[4]It may be noted that hydraulic energy, solar (which includes the energy latent in winds and tides), thermonuclear, volcanic and geothermal energy sources are nonpollutant, unlike the use of coal, oil and atomic energy. The disposal of nuclear wastes has, however, become a controversial problem of magnitude.

Part III
The Industrialization of Black Africa

The joint concentration of energy sources and raw materials determines the existence of eight natural zones for industrial development in Black Africa.

1) The Zaire River Basin

With its 650 billion kilowatt-hours of annual reserves of hydraulic energy (almost two-thirds of world production) the Zaire River Basin is destined to become the leading industrial region of Africa, the principal center of our heavy industry. In the final stage, hydraulic energy will supply all the electricity needed for the various branches of industry using the resources of raw materials in neighboring territories: the coking coal of South Africa and Southern Rhodesia (Zimbabwe), the iron of Angola and even Zaire, cobalt (65 percent of world production); chromium (one third of world production); tantalium (85 percent of world production in Nigeria alone); cadmium, vanadium, manganese, tin, copper (overlapping from Upper Shaba into Zambia), the richest ore in the world; zinc, lead, silver, industrial diamonds, gold, uranium (the Shinkrolobwe mines, top exporter in the world, 60 to 70 percent of total mined).[1]

The simultaneous abundance of hydraulically created electricity and nonferrous metals makes the region especially suited to the fabrication of specialized steels for strategic or domestic uses, having numerous industrial applications: chromium steels (armor, corrosion-resistant), chromium-wolfram-cobalt steels (for rapid cutting), silicum steel (industrial uses, dynamos), cobalt steel (for the manufacture of permanent magnets, because of the large coercive field they may hold: 300 oerstads), tantalium steels (high-temperature resistant), magnesium steels (shock resistant).

Only regions privileged in electric power can specialize in the production of such electrosteels (refined in electric furnaces). The same is true of electrometallurgical industry in general for the handling of by-products of copper ores (lead, tin, silver), refinement of that metal or zinc, tin or lead, manufacture of electrolytic iron, of magnesium through electrolysis of sea water, extraction of heavy hydrogen from such water, at a later date when thermonuclear energy has been brought under control.

This region is as privileged as Canada for the handling of bauxite from other countries and the creation of an aluminothermal industry. Eventual discovery of iron ores with a yield above 25 percent and bauxite would give this country an indisputable primacy for the location of heavy industry.

Thanks to light alloys, the Atlantic coast seems a good prospect for a center of aerospace construction. Likewise, our steelmills would supply naval, automobile, farm combine and other such production centers. Zaire might even export sheetmetal and tubing to other eventual naval or aeronautical construction centers, such as Dakar, Mombasa or others.

Its virgin forest also makes it a favored site for the creation of a varied lumber industry, from plywood to the chemical distillation of wood with its derivatives (methyl alcohol, acetone, tar, cyclical derivatives that may serve as the raw material for synthesis in a dye industry), a woodpulp industry and manmade fabrics from cellulose, plastics and so on—all coming out of the forest. Thanks to the use of specially selected noncarcinogenic insecticides, Equatorial Africa will be the coming cattle-raising region with immense year-round green prairies.

The other industrial vegetation cultivated in Zaire, oleaginous plants (palm trees), hevea (rubber), cotton, sugar cane, coffee, cacao, give some idea of the multiplicity of industries which would necessarily concentrate in this region: tires (using rubber and cotton, the latter supplying the fabric, while the sulfur resulting from zinc-smelting for armorplating would be used to vulcanize the rubber or else to produce sulfuric acid); in the same way, there·would be sugarmills and refineries, spinning and weaving mills and oil/soap production. Some of these industries are already extant in the region but only in the most sporadic manner; they are merely complementary industries, quite inadequate to satisfy the needs of the African continent, let alone provide a surplus for export.

Once having supplied all of these industries, the excess electrical energy of the Zaire River Basin could serve as a seasonal supplement for the other regions of Africa, especially the tropical ones, through an interconnection of grids. This would, of course, presuppose an understanding among the various African territories before the first of these installations was made, standardizing of certain norms, such as the cycle of current to be produced, and so on.

While our major share of uranium comes from this region and South Africa (which also has significant thorium deposits), it would be absurd to create nuclear power plants here in the future, since there are such large quantities of other energy: hydraulic and perhaps petroleum. Nuclear and thermal plants, in general, should be restricted to regions which are apparently lacking in other energy sources (but in the meantime we will stockpile radioactive wastes, pending future study). I say "apparently lacking," because it is almost certain that systematic oil exploration currently under way in tropical Africa (Senegal, Sudan, Niger and southern Sahara) will completely alter the energy picture in those regions. This seems especially true in Senegal and the Ivory Coast. Moreover, we are far from having exhausted the possibilities of nonprohibitive hydroelectric plant-building in the tropics, whatever the level of the waterways.

Zaire might create a significant chemical industry (various fertilizers), a synthetic chemistry industry and cement works. The latter could call upon local clays and chalks and the noncoking coals of other regions (Nigeria and Tanzania with its more than 7 billion metric tons in reserves).

Systematic development of rice growing in Zaire, Nigeria, Dahomey (Benin), south Togo, Ivory Coast, Guinea, the Casamance, Senegal and Niger valleys, Sudan, around Lake Chad and elsewhere as well as in East Africa must be carried out in such a way as totally to change eating habits on the continent, replacing millet with rice as the basic dietary staple. In a near future, in three vital areas—food (rice), clothing (cottongoods), housing (cement and concrete)—Africa will be able to forego its dependence on the outside by ceasing imports from either Asia or Europe.

Industrial shark fishing (for vitamin oils) and whaling in the Gabon region is famous. The well-stocked fisheries of the African West Coast are generally in contrast to those of Europe, which are becoming increasingly depleted. We can anticipate a national fishing industry up and down the African coast, especially in Zaire. We must not overlook freshwater fishing in view of the density of fish in the Zaire River and the canning industry that is its counterpart. Here again, tin smelting would provide the necessary containers, as it would for other canned foods, such as equatorial fruits. A special refrigeration or ice industry will be developed or created correlatively throughout equatorial and tropical Africa.

In an almost dramatic contradiction, the Zaire River Basin today holds almost all of our continental wealth while being the least populous area of the continent. It has 19 million people against 14 million in the Sahara, with a density of only two to three per square kilometer. This makes the region as rich as it is deserted, virtually as deserted as the desert itself

This internal weakness will have to be remedied in the future by a policy of hygiene and systematic birth encouragement, that is, an appropriate demographic policy, excluding any massive influx of foreigners or import of a foreign labor force. For the immediate future, the first years of industrialization, a selective resort to manpower from neighboring African territories should be sufficient, since mechanization of agriculture and automation will be able to make up for some of the manpower shortage.

Our notion of optimum populations must be revised. It does not mean the same thing it did before automation. However that may be, the problem of repopulating Africa, of reconstituting its population decimated by slavery far beyond the toll of what has often been attributed to illness, remains an acute problem for all Africans.

Zaire and the Congo, with a large part of Equatorial Africa, form a unified natural zone with the same economic characteristics. That is why I made no effort artificially to differentiate between the two banks of the Zaire in an overview such as this.

The importance of the Zaire Basin is undeniable for all Africans, especially for us French-speaking Africans, who are more likely than our comrades of English, Portuguese or other tutelage to enter into direct relations with the population of this territory with a view to establishing permanent links among our peoples so we may build our common future together. All the countries of Africa should participate in the industrial development of this region, in particular in the construction of the Inga Dam, which was projected to produce 400 billions kilowatts per annum in Zaire.

2) The Gulf of Benin Region

The region with Nigeria (the Niger delta) at its center, bordered by Dahomey (Benin) and Togo on the west and Cameroon on the east, is also a future industrial center.

Its hydraulic reserves total 250 billion kilowatt-hours (200 in maritime Sanga, 50 in Nigeria). Moreover, oil has just been discovered in Gabon; all existing indications point to oil becoming a significant factor among the various sources of energy that will industrialize the country.

We have already said that Nigeria has a monopoly of tantalum. It also has tin, noncoking coal and immense reserves of lignite, amounting to some 200 million metric tons. Cameroon produces uranium, tin and gold. There is already an aluminum industry in the area, thanks to the Edea Dam. It would be proper to encourage development here of a powerful electrosmelting, electrochemical and chemical industry, the last of these making use of low-grade coal as a raw material for synthetics.

All of southern Nigeria, Togo and Dahomey although very humid has been deforested to permit planting. Dense forest has disappeared there, but there is still such forest in seaside Cameroon in the basin of the Sanga River. There the possibility still exists of seeing the growth of a powerful wood chemical industry: distillation, pulp, manmade fabrics.

Low-grade coal could also be used in some of the thermal plants to the north. The presence of oil palms, cocoanut trees (copra), hevea in Camerooon, sugar cane and cacao, permits creation of the corresponding industries: oil/soap works, tire factories using local cotton for fabric base, sugarmills and refineries, etc. The cultivation of rice as a food staple could systematically be developed in the delta region.

3) *Ghana and the Ivory Coast*

These two countries jointly have 25 billion annual kilowatt-hours in energy reserves, once harnessing the Upper Volta, Bandama and Comoe rivers is complete. Ghana's suitability for the development of an aluminothermal industry is obvious: bauxite is abundant close by the hydraulic energy. Ghana entered the era of aluminothermy in 1970, producing 157,200 metric tons of aluminum in 1974. The Akosombo Dam produced 3,304,000 kilowatt-hours of hydroelectric power in 1972.

Manganese, on which Ghana has a virtual African monopoly, might find appropriate local use in electroplating if systematic exploration by plane or other methods revealed the presence of iron and nonferrous metals in Ghana and the Ivory Coast. Even in that case, Ghana would be better advised to import coal from South Africa, Rhodesia or even from Europe rather than to take advantage of the proximity of the Ivorian forest, which is dense forest, to try to make wood steel. Absolute lack of coal alone would justify recourse to such a method which, if I may say so, would be barbaric.

Even in Equatorial Africa, in the Congo where dense forest is dominant, I cannot envisage such a course. Our forest, especially that of the Ivory Coast, must be reserved for essentially chemical utilization, and the Ivory Coast is especially suited for housing such a forest-based chemical industry on the same basis as the two regions mentioned earlier with the same variations: a wood industry in all its aspects.

Ghana and the Ivory Coast together account for more than half the world's production of cacao. The gold of the Ivory Coast, Ghana and Cameroon and the diamonds of Zaire and Angola are destined to have special application.[2]

The wealth of the Ivory Coast until now has been essentially agricultural. Throughout this region there is the possibility of setting up canneries for fruits and vegetables (pineapples, bananas, cacao, yams), oil/soap plants and of fostering intensive rice-growing.

4) Guinea, Sierra Leone, Liberia

This is a metallurgical region par excellence, ideal for the installation of a powerful combine, as several authors have already pointed out. Indeed, it has more than 25 billion annual kilowatt-hours of hydraulic energy reserves. The Konkouré Dam in lower Guinea is expected to deliver 200,000 kilowatts of power.

The iron ore of the Kalum peninsula has a yield of 50 percent. It is estimated to reach 2 billion metric tons. The bauxite of the Loos Islands in Guinea is estimated at 10 million metric tons. Bauxite is also found, disseminated here and there, in other regions as far as Upper Guinea. To these ores we should add the iron of Liberia (Boni Hills). There are also industrial diamonds and uranium in the Macenta. This whole region, from Liberia to Guinea, is good for raising hevea.

By importing coal, a powerful metallurgical industry could be developed here along with aluminothermy and tire factories, which is to say that the region is a future center for the automotive and aerospace industries (planes, ballistic missiles, interplanetary rockets and the rest). It could also accommodate oil/soap works, since it has oil palms and other oleaginous flora, and canneries for such fruits as bananas and pineapples.

It would lend itself well to intensive cultivation of rice, cola nuts and as in the Ivory Coast spices, coffee and indigo.

5) Tropical Zone (Senegal, Mali, Niger)

These regions are supposed to be energy-deficient, but such an unfavorable reputation does not mean we cannot look beyond appearances to see what industrial future they might conceivably have. Oil exploration, being carried out more and more systematically in the South Sahara, will in all likelihood totally change the energy picture in these heretofore seemingly energyless tropical regions. Petroleum would supply both the indispensable energy source for the establishment of thermal power plants and the necessary raw materials for a petrochemical industry. Everyone is aware of the line of products and by-products extracted or synthesized from petroleum derivatives (fertilizers, pharmaceuticals, plastics, insecticides, synthetic rubber, manmade fabrics and so on). The abundance of hydroelectric power in other African regions (especially the Equatorial) has led to minimizing the hydroelectrical potential of Senegal and Mali in particular.

If we look at the industrialization of these regions and their energy development within an overall plan, Africawide, the setting-up of certain industries as the exploitation of certain energy sources becomes ridiculous if not absurd, at least within the first phase of a general industrialization. Only in case of a kind of industrial autarchy (if Senegal and Mali could not readily reach understanding with the other territories) could one foresee the setting-up of, say, a micro-metallurgy at Kédougou.

Otherwise, mutual concessions permitting not only interconnection of power distribution lines but also industrial specialization of different areas, Senegal and Mali would have to move resolutely toward the establishment of powerful textile, cement, petroleum and fishing industries.[3]

The Senegal River valley, the Macina region and the bend of the Niger would be laid out according to the old Niger

Office Project for intensive cotton raising (at the same time as rice).

In the tropical and equatorial regions of the world, and especially Africa, it can be forecast that hygiene and climate considerations will keep synthetic fabrics from ever totally displacing cottongoods for clothing.[4] The two tropical zones of Africa on either side of the Equator could be turned into textile-producing zones not only for domestic consumption but also for export.

Textiles: A peculiarity of the textile industry is that its equipment is robust and may last up to half a century, but it quickly becomes out of date. That is why the textile industries of old countries with timeworn equipment (especially France) have been left behind by the industries of younger countries with ultramodern highly mechanized machinery. Japan and India are now exporting cotton goods even to Black Africa.

An entire spinning and weaving industry will have to be set up so that it can produce not only apparel cotton but also jute and sisal for packing (peanut shipping-sacks). This means that jute- and sisal-raising would also have to be considered with shortages to be made up by imports from Zaire and Tanzania.

There would also be the weaving of artificial fibers, based on the wood-chemistry plants of the Casamance (see below). Likewise fabrics manufactured in the north might eventually become the textile base for tires made in the Casamance factories from the product of the hevea plantations. The textile industry employs mainly womanpower (50 to 60 percent), which makes it good for a total-employment program, and beyond that it could bring new life to cities such as St.-Louis-du-Sénégal.

Dyes: This industry goes right along with that of textiles, so Senegal and Mali would have to develop it at the same time. This tropical region should, therefore, become the site of a veritable African IG Farbenindustrie.

In view of the abundance of energy resources in Black Africa, it seems less and less necessary to manufacture synthetic fuels from low-grade coals (e.g., gasoline extracted by the Fischer-Trops process). A chemical-dye industry in our regions would be the natural beneficiary of Nigeria's low-grade coal as raw material from which the needed cyclical derivatives could be distilled for use in printing the fabrics. In reality, so powerful an industry might easily diversify to various areas of synthetic consumer products.

Cement: The African market is as insatiable for cement as for textiles, if not more so. The entire Senegalese coast, with chalk and clay found everywhere,[5] could develop a first-magnitude cement industry. All that would be needed is coal from Nigeria, Tanzania, South Africa or even Europe for firing the ovens. There could also be brickworks and tileworks, likewise glassworks using the sands of the beaches and elsewhere. Glass is nothing but a silicate of sodium, and its manufacture is a simple chemical process.

The day when enough oil has been found in the territories of Senegal, Mali or Niger or in the Sahara, the problem of heating the furnaces will be solved: oil replacing coal.[6]

Oil seeds: The oil-palm forests, growing wild from the Casamance to St.-Louis-du-Sénégal by way of the region of the Niayes, could supply significant oil/soap factories at Ziguinchor, in the Djander, at St.-Louis, beyond those already in existence at Dakar, which currently process two-thirds of the peanut production of Senegal. Peanut-raising can be increased with little human effort by substituting an intensive method for the extensive one, using fertilizers and mechanization (pickers, thresher/crackers, collecting stations and so on). African oileries making peanut oil have ceased using imported coal and replaced it by coke. And the oilcakes are used for feeding cattle.

The castor-oil plant can be raised generally, since it furnishes a highly appreciated industrial oil, among other reasons because it can withstand high temperatures without igniting (as in airplane motors, for example).

Increased cotton-raising would, of course, provide additional oil to be processed from the seeds.

Fishing: In years to come, it will be seen that an entire deepsea fishing fleet will be needed off the coasts of Senegal to reap maximum industrial benefits from the banks of fish and shellfish in these regions. The fisheries of Port-Étienne are well known for their lobsters and tuna, and European fishermen (primarily from Brittany), whose coasts are losing their supply of fish, spend months each year all along the Atlantic coasts of Africa.

There are a great many sharks off Dakar, and this fish, as is known, gives a high-vitamin oil of much value in pharmacy.

A fleet, if well equipped, might go down as far as Pointe-Noire off Gabon and even try its hand at whaling, which is industrially profitable. Detailed scientific studies have shown that regions of the African coast would prove fruitful. All sorts of by-product industries could grow out of the catch, from canneries to margarine factories to pharmaceutical enterprises.

An ice industry supported by solar energy or other sources of energy would make available fresh fish not only in the coastal regions but in the interior as well the year round.

Wood Chemistry: For lack of concluding an agreement, southern Senegal (the Casamance) will have to develop a wood-chemical industry that would be superfluous under other circumstances.

The Casamance is a relatively wooded humid region, but really dense forest, characteristic of Equatorial Africa, is found there only in isolated spots. To supply a wood-chemistry industry, considering the weak annual new growth in our forests (.22 square meters on an average), scientific reforestation will be required. In order to renew the forest in optimum time, it may even be necessary, as has been advised in other regions, to concentrate on quick-growing plants (cactuses or even annuals such as papyrus). The golden rule in the economies of Mali and Senegal must be never to deforest the smallest piece of land. Deforestation of the Casamance in order to make way for wider peanut-planting by private companies is a national catastrophe. The spaces available in the north (as outlined above) are more than sufficient for raising this oil-seed if new and scientific methods are applied.

The Casamance, methodically reforested, might supply the raw material for a wood-chemical industry, set up on its own territory, say, in the suburbs of Ziguinchor. It would produce pulp, paper for internal consumption (newspapers, stationery, printing), textile fibers for use in weaving factories in Senegal and the Niger bend, and raw materials for match and explosives factories. The distillation of wood would yield tars, cyclical derivatives for the dye works, methyl alcohol, acetone and so on for local chemical synthesis.

The Casamance might, moreover, return to rubber-raising, discontinued around 1910 to make way for peanuts, and likewise to sugar cane with a view to creating sugar refineries.

Hevea culture, resumed with a methodical, scientific plan, would make the Casamance the southern tip of the natural-rubber zone that extends from the Ivory Coast by way of

Liberia and Guinea. The tire industry would be set up in the region and might help relieve the load of the Guinea-Sierra Leone complex.

Whatever may be said, the new synthetic processes are far from having dethroned natural rubber, for the question of getting raw materials has not been satisfactorily resolved. The new process for synthesizing rubber uses isoprene as raw material and lithium as a catalyst. This gives the same regular pattern of methyl radicals on either side of the main chain as in natural hevea. The cost of the basic isoprene is low enough to allow competition with natural rubber to a point. For decades to come, it will remain absurd for a continent as favorable as Africa is to hevea plantations to turn its attention to synthesizing natural rubber.

In the truck-gardening areas, such as Bargny near Rufisque, Tivaouane, Diourbel, Kaolack, Ziguinchor, there could be large and varied food canneries (mangoes, guavas, pineapples, etc.).

Senegal could also extend its specialization in the chemical industry by setting up fertilizer factories using phosphates (Taïba), potassium and nitrates to supply various agricultural zones of Africa.

Rice: The old project for domestication of the lower valley of the Senegal River called for highwater fillings of the Lac de Guiers so that at low water these stored reserves could be used to desalinate the river's banks. This would allow for planting fifty thousand hectares (125,000 acres) of rice. We might add that such a reserve water supply upon its release for agricultural purposes (and even when flowing in) might serve as motor force for crushing cereals (millet and others) in industrial mills (the lake is approximately 50 by 10 kilometers, or 31 by 6 miles). The other no less old project, the Niger Office (1932), also planned to provide about a million hectares for cotton and rice, partly in the Niger bend (Lake Debo region) and partly in the interior delta (Macina) between the Niger and the Bani rivers.

Raising rice, as cotton, requires abundant manpower, so that before the day of mechanization Asia with its population density virtually monopolized rice production.

We have already pointed out that automation and mechanization today are totally changing the concept of optimum population and that relatively meagerly populated regions (such as Senegal or Mali), if they adopt new scientific methods as well as a repopulation policy, might be able to get by, thanks to extreme mechanization of agriculture and as great automation as possible of the final-stage industries. Rice must replace millet in the national diet.

Entirely automated oil-production centers have been built in the Volga Basin, remote-controlled by one central headquarters, and have quintupled the Soviet Union's petroleum output.

At Dartmoor, England, the first totally automated powerplant in the world, run by controls almost a hundred miles away, has been in operation since 1960.

Reforestation: The Sahel zone, the more desert the farther north one goes, is ideal for reforestation. As early as 1950, we suggested a plan for replanting here. Although approved at the time by the Senegalese people and taken under consideration by the administration, this plan has since lain dormant.

The methods used in the southern USSR (Voronezh) to recreate moisture in the region would be greatly useful to us. We ought to draw maximum lessons from them before today undertaking reforestation of the Sahel on a continentwide scale. Man can recreate humus of his own on arid sand.

However evident Mali's suitability for chemical and textile industries and rice-raising may be, the last word has not yet been spoken. In a later phase, if the unification of Africa were to meet with sufficient temporary difficulties, Senegal might set up its own heavy industry by importing coking coal for the smelting of iron from Mauritania (50 million metric tons of reserves at Iron Mountain near Fort-Gouraud) and from its own Kédougou.

Copper from the same region could be processed with the hydroelectric power generated by the Gouina Dam, which we shall presently discuss. Titanum, found in abundance in the coastal sands (Casamance, Rufisque, Petite Côte), with other nonferrous metals could form a base for the smelting of light alloys that in the future with the growing importance of aeronautics and astronautics will take on capital significance.

It is also important to mention the main future source of materials for metallurgy, the recycling of all sorts of old iron. Obviously, as different metal mines begin to be exhausted, recycling of old metals will increasingly become a prime source of supply. In the years before World War II, German heavy industry (Krupp and Thyssen) was kept going in large part through such recycling; in other words, many of Hitler's tanks and armored ships were constructed from recycled materials. We can still remember the ships that stood off Dakar for weeks on end, buying scrap—even in lots as small as a kilogram—collected by idlers, children and the unemployed.

For this resource, which even now is most significant, Senegal is as well off as any territory. For the present the main source must remain the pure iron of Mauritania, and the natural refinery for that is in Senegal. To establish a refining complex in Mauritania, either by extracting fresh water from the sea and piping the desalinated water hundreds of miles inland or doing the necessary digging and installation of wells in appropriate places to reach the fresh-water lake that underlies the Sahara[7], even apart from other improvements required in this desert region without up-country, would be prohibitive.

However that may be, Dakar's future as a principal port for air and sea construction can clearly be seen. With or without local heavy industry, Dakar in the future, thanks to its privileged location and the shelter it affords, must become one of the main African centers of naval construction, importing sheet-iron pressed in the neighboring complexes of Guinea and Zaire.[8]

While Dakar continues to develop, some of the many industries enumerated above, especially textiles and dyes, would be set up at St.-Louis and would restore life to that old capital with its delightful abundance of neglected womanpower.

Cattle: The skinniness of livestock in the Sahel region (Senegal and Mali) is proverbial. A cow gives a tenth the milk she would in Europe. The irrigation ditches that will be dug to bring water from the rivers will permit, in addition to rice and cotton planting, the raising of grazing plants and the creation of manmade prairies for the cattle. Their droppings in turn will supply a complete fertilizer, containing nitrogen, potassium and phosphate, the three mineral elements that vegetation is constantly sapping out of the soil.

Similarly, other by-products of the future food industry will serve systematically as cattle fodder: oilcakes, fruit pulps from the canneries, and so on. While there are no tse-tse flies, neither are there any prairies in those areas to the north. Windmills will be needed, not only to produce electricity but also to bring water for the cattle in Ferlo to drink, for irrigation and for making tobacco crops possible. In the Casamance, dusting with insecticides by plane will be required to wipe out the tse-tses. A study of the marketing of certain flora with industrial potential will also be a must.

Energy problems: On the Senegal River resumption of planning and construction of the huge Gouina Dam in Mali upstream from Cayes is imperative. The site was chosen, among other reasons, probably because this part of the riverbed is still on that old shelf where less water is lost to infiltration than in sedimentary terrain. The dam was to allow for irrigation of all the upper valley for cotton and rice, to regulate the flow of the river seasonally for navigation and at the same time to produce an enormous quantity of electric power, the future application of which need not concern us today.

Interconnecting the grid of high-tension powerlines carrying electricity produced by the waterfall at plants below the dam with lines coming from remote thermal powerplants on the Atlantic coast or in Mali would pose no special technical transport problem. The distances involved are relatively small, often smaller than those between French powerplants. The electrical power available after construction of the Gouina Dam alone would in itself be enough to feed all the industries of Mali and Senegal that we have outlined in this study.

Farther down the Senegal River Valley, since the flow is so irregular as water seeps away in the calcareous terrain, one would have to consider the feasibility of constructing a dam at Dagana as well as micro-generators strung out along the river's course down to the lower valley. The creation of large reservoirs would allow these to operate even in low-water periods. It would remain to be determined whether the addition of such reservoirs would be more economical than construction of the micro-generators without reservoirs, supplying supplemental power only at certain periods of the year and the rest of the time operating at something like one-hundredth of their potential capacity. The flow of the Senegal varies, to be sure, from ten cubic meters at its lowest to four thousand to five thousand cubic meters at its crest. The water rises at such periods to twelve meters (almost forty feet). Similarly, the feasibility of dams on the Upper Gambia and Casamance rivers will have to be studied, since these two waterways have until now been overlooked, hydroelectrically speaking.

In the final stage, there will also be occasion to study the feasibility of tidal generators at the mouth of the Senegal. Sea waters here ride in as far as Dagana and Podor, representing a volume of several millions of cubic meters, which nature shuffles back and forth in the flow and ebb of each tide. There is nothing absurd in the idea of mechanically harnessing this tidal energy into electric power rather than letting it dissipate in thin air as it does now.

Indeed, the three factors involved—unit of height, tidal coefficient and establishment of the port—are no less favorable here than in certain spots on the French coast which are considered the best in the world. A chart of tidal ranges (twice the product of the unit of height by the tidal coefficient or factor) shows 5.4 for Africa's west coast at the level of the Senegal River as against 4.6 for the Bay of Arcachon and the mouth of the Garonne, 5.4 for the Bay of La Rochelle, 5.2 for the mouth of the Loire and 6.4 in the Finistère (Brittany). The small tidal ranges of other points on the African Atlantic coast (1.6 in the Gulf of Guinea) rule them out as locations for such projects.

Only in the estuaries on the English Channel, which constitutes a special kind of resonance basin, do these ranges reach greater heights, almost rivaling those of Canada[9]: 11.4 for the estuary of the Rance and 12.5 for the Bay of Mont-St.-Michel, both in Brittany.

The abundance of favorable sites in France and the huge

costs involved in installing tidal powerplants, according to Robert Gibrat, have led the French government to drop plans for any plants of lesser power. The problem is analogous to that for the harnessing of waterfalls. It can be summed up in two factors: the mass of water involved and the height of the drop under which it is to be handled. The latter factor is the one that for our coasts is slight, while the former (in this case, the stretch of the basins) is extremely high.

Along the same lines, it would be good to consider the possibility of harnessing the estuary of the Sine-Salum, where the sea drives in as much as seventy kilometers (almost forty miles) at Kaoleck, and those of the Gambia and Casamance, in which the sea also reaches tens of kilometers inland. Hydroelectric plants set up there would be equipped with double-action turbines, operating both at influx and at outflow. Such installations are expensive, and we will have to be content to start with thermal plants while building Gouina.

We know that a certain minimum drop is required for the motive force of water to be transformed into turbine-generated electricity. If after study it turned out that this fundamental condition were not satisfied by the estuaries of our rivers, we might try without much conviction to compensate for this major drawback by:

a) siphoning into higher and higher basins, as is already planned in the English Channel projects (Rance and Mont-St.-Michel);
b) building underground works that would operate by the direct action of water ebbing at low tide.

We must not overlook the fact that tidal power is only a supplemental source of energy for Black Africa. It is not included in the calculations that give our continent half of the world's leading energy-rich countries. That classification has not changed one iota; the picture is still optimistic.

It was only in order to effect a complete inventory that we considered this complementary, truly secondary, indeed hypothetical source of energy. Let no one misjudge its relative importance.

In the immediate future, powerplants in Black Africa will most likely use coal, in view of the proximity of this fuel.[10] In the second stage, we could set up diesel generators, using heavy oil, as soon as sufficient oil strikes have been made in Mali and Senegal. At the same time, we could produce power from natural gas. Finally, as we develop technical expertise, we will in a not-distant future set up atomic plants using plutonium. We will resolutely orient ourselves toward breeder reactors, which have the greatest potential. We need not repeat that these reactors perform a kind of industrial miracle: as they operate, they throw off more fuel (plutonium) than they have consumed. Such an operation presupposes the simultaneous creation of plutonium-producing piles fed by natural enriched uranium. For the first time, plutonium would be put to use for peaceful purposes.

Future African reactors will of course have to stockpile their waste, the solid wastes at least, until serious studies allow us to determine the best way to dispose of them. The English method, in which wastes are piped down to the bottom of the sea, is absolutely to be ruled out.

Solar energy could as of now be employed for home use by relatively modest methods. In India, the National Physical Laboratory of Delhi has perfected different types of solar cookers, often parabolic in shape. They are practical for the preparation of medium-sized meals. Further perfecting the process and popularizing the use of solar cookers might lead to their adoption as domestic labor-saving devices that would significantly contribute to conservation of the few forests left. To the extent that such kitchen ranges were in use, we would see a drop in the unobtrusive, but nonetheless intense and disastrous, deforestation practiced by dealers in dead wood, the Laobés and others.

In France, there is the campers' solar cooker created by N. Doumé. Maria Telkes's model can reach 100° Centigrade (212° Fahrenheit), according to Félix Trombes. Solar energy could be used in water heaters and air-conditioned homes, for distilling water and for freezing, in a coil using the solution and liquefaction of ammonia under eight atmospheres at ordinary temperature.

Félix Trombes believes we can anticipate low-level (5 percent) solar motors delivering mechanical energy that can be used to produce cold with an efficiency of 300 percent, utilizing the principle of the refrigeration cycle (that is, Carnot's cycle operating in reverse). On an industrial scale, nothing immediate can be expected; at present, solar-driven motors are too costly, and Trombes estimates that installation would come to between half a million and a million old francs per kilowatt. As for its direct application, he could then see two possible means, either a reduction in cost of low-yield machines or construction of high yield ones that would allow for the use of turbines.

It seems the Italians have attempted to commercialize a motor fueled with vaporized fluids, such as liquid and gaseous sulfur anhydride.

It will be recalled that experiments had been made in Egypt in 1912 by Schumann of Philadelphia, using cylindrico-parabolic mirrors and working at reduced pressure; he succeeded in generating fifty horsepower and an efficiency yield of about 5 percent. But that plant, set up at Maadi, was abandoned in 1914.

Before making this industrial attempt, Schumann had experimented in the laboratory, as it were, by combining reduced pressure with a hothouse effect, surrounding a flat boiler with a vitreous cuff. It is a fact that light rays penetrating a glass enclosure, after being reflected by the object within, take on greater wave lengths that come close to the hot radiations of infrared light and, as a result, no longer can escape from the enclosure. Since the wave length has been increased, the glass becomes impermeable, hermetic so to speak, in relation to them. The consequent accumulation of energy raises the temperature, creating the "hothouse effect."

Our goal, in thus referring to the technical details of certain past efforts, is to show eventual young African researchers the perspectives that are open to them.

Finally, according to du Jonchay, the site of Cayar in the Diander by the sea is a good one for the installation of a hydrothermal generating plant of the type now being set up at Abidjan.

6) Nilotic Sudan, Great Lakes, Ethiopia

This region, several times as large as Europe, has its principal energy source in the reserves of the Nile and its tributaries: potentially more than 60 billion kilowatt-hours per year. The major part of this energy is to be furnished by the dam at Oven at the issue of Lake Victoria. There are also uranium deposits.

The port of Mombasa in Kenya on the Indian Ocean is due to become a great naval-construction center.

Growing cotton, sugar cane, hemp, sisal, oil palms and cocoanut trees (in the coastal plain) calls for setting-up of corresponding industries. On the other hand, maize and other cereals, coffee and tea, are grown for consumption and export.

The country is equally well suited to sizable cattle spreads in the savannah. It has the whole range of climatic zones, right on up to the snows of the Mountains of the Moon.

Many of the sites that appeal to tourists would also be ideal for the establishment of sanitariums and rest homes.

7) Zambezi River Basin

The energy potential here, according to figures published by du Jonchay, is 45 billion kilowatt-hours annually. Again, there are uranium deposits.

Du Jonchay calls the coal basin of the Wankie in Zimbabwe with its coking coals Africa's largest reserve. The basin of the Ruhuhu River in Tanganyika has 6.5 billion metric tons of coal reserves.

In Southwest Africa, there are vanadium deposits enough to feed smelters of resistant steel for aeronautics and electrical construction. With the huge Kabora-Bassa Dam and the iron ore this region has, it can be considered an African Ruhr Basin.

8) *Union of South Africa*

This country has already been industrialized by its European minority inhabitants. It has gold, diamonds, coking coal (in Transvaal, Natal), uranium, thorium (at the Cape) and wool of international quality from merino sheep.

There is prosperous sugar-cane raising on the Indian Ocean coast, and it would appear that the Kalahari Desert at its northern border is as oil-rich as the Sahara.

Transport

In a first phase, all of the above calls for the building of modern highways, transcontinental blacktop or concrete expressways and strong civil air lines.

The building of new railroads, considering the difficulties involved, may be postponed until later. On the other hand, all specialists agree on the importance of the hydroplane as a method of internal travel over Africa, in view of the many lakes and waterways available. Hydroplanes and helicopters would be especially useful for middle-distance travel, and they then would in no way interfere with high-speed commercial air transport. What must be pointed out here is the absurdity from an economic viewpoint in a new country like Africa of a policy of railroad-building in the initial stage of development. Those railroads that prove indispensable after thorough study will be necessarily electric-powered or at least diesel-fueled and will come into being along with the development of electrical power and the exploitation of petroleum.

As for sea transport, we will later build only a minimum of luxury liners for ocean tourism, but the whole continent will devote its efforts to the construction of high-tonnage freighters (forty thousand tons minimum): tankers, banana boats, gas tankers and so on.

This seems worth delineating right now, for it is important from the start to establish a technical and industrial doctrine that will eschew present and future trial-and-error and the costly luxury of false starts.

Training Key Personnel

To begin our industrialization, we will first import prefabricated factories with trained foreign personnel who are accustomed to using the machinery, having conceived and tested it. Such factories may fall into every category; heavy-metal industries, chemistry, electronics, etc., all as automated as possible.

We know that an African technician placed in optimum conditions of responsibility must and can quickly assimilate the knowledge needed so that he in turn can direct a whole complex on which the life of the nation, or in due time the life of the whole continent, will depend. When the moment comes, we will have to be ready to place African technicians squarely before their responsibilities. In other words, they will have to be ready in the shortest possible time to replace foreign technicians at their machines and with their tools.

When this first industrial infrastructure has been set up, we will have to establish assembly plants for various machines and implements: tractors, planes, automobiles, what have you.

At the same time, we must acquire foreign patents for the production under license of our first modern engines and machines: motors, various modern propulsion systems (turbo-reactors), electronic apparatus and more.

This period will be as brief as possible so that Africans may rapidly go on to the phase of autonomous native technical construction and accomplishments.

Second-level personnel will be trained in large part right on the job, in factories, shops and on work sites.

[1]These uranium reserves have been since exhausted, by intense extraction; part of the ore is very probably being stored at Oolen, Belgium.

[2]See: *Conclusion, Investment Funds*

[3]First there has to be nationwide access to power; then later research will lead toward the transport of energy by direct current (as in the Switzerland-Germany-Italy complex).

[4]Unless chemistry, that wonderworking fairy of the industrial era, one day develops an artificial fiber with all the good properties of cotton.

[5]Tertiary calcareous rock and marns along the whole coast from Dakar to Joal.

[6]An enlightened economic policy should systematically favor petroleum exploration under given conditions.

[7]A fifth of the whole Saharan surface is said to overlie fresh water, at twelve hundred to fourteen hundred meters depth, in the Albien.

[8]The Dakar-Marine project appears since to have borne this out.

[9]The world's greatest tidal ranges are in the joint Canadian-American Bay of Fundy, 16 meters (almost 53 feet) and Passamaquoddy Bay, 15 meters. Three other Canadian sites have ranges exceeding 12 meters. *(Translator's Note)*

[10]Barring the creation of an African common market for coal, fuel oil remains most practical. The study, mastery and organization of our internal African market, a determining component of the world market, is an urgent task.

Conclusion

To this point, I have traced a general outline of industrialization in the absolute without bringing out the rhythm to be adopted so that it might be realized, nor establishing any close correlation between it and actual present possibilities. It goes without saying that there have been certain sporadic industrial accomplishments at various spots on the continent, but there has been no overall plan, for reasons easy to see. There could be none prior to political unification or at least establishment of multilateral agreements. However that may be, even such limited industrialization cannot be crowned with success unless there be participation of the State and the people as a whole.

Investment Funds

In all that has gone before, we have tried to show, contrary to current assumptions, that the continent does have an industrial destiny. We have especially underlined the fact that the economic and industrial future of Mali (that is, the old Senegal-Sudan Federation) will necessarily be prosperous, whatever pessimistic prophets may say, if industrializing efforts resolutely take the direction we have indicated. We must note, having made this overall absolute appraisal, the real investment means available now to prepare so vast an enterprise.

Where would risk capital come from? There are five sources for it:

1.   At the beginning we would have to adopt a NEP (New Economic Policy, adopted by Lenin in 1921) of our own. Repeating this old Russian economic experiment will have to be surrounded by the greatest precautions; at the very least, right from the start companies would have to be jointly owned and operated with the State's share constantly increasing.

Within the framework we have traced, we now have to define areas of investment for private companies. Instead of letting them come into the country with their teams of technicians to evaluate its treasures and then freely select among them what they think would prove most lucrative for their investment, the State—basing its decisions on the needs of its own industrialization plan—must put a brake on such anarchy by holding the reins of economic development.

2.   For hard currencies and machinery we would exchange our precious metals, gold, silver, and platinum: what is left of old gold and the ores of the Bambouk and the Falémé, the N'Galam in Senegal and Mali; the gold of Ghana, Cameroon, Zaire, the Ivory Coast, Guinea; the gold of Central and East Africa and Rhodesia and the Union of South Africa, once the continent has been unified on the basis of our own supremacy.

The same applies to the diamonds of Guinea, Cameroon, Angola, Zaire, Tanzania and South Africa.

3.   We would sell our excess strategic raw materials, as long as our own industry could not absorb them: manganese from Zaire, Ghana, Ivory Coast, South Africa and Cameroon; tantalum of Nigeria; titanium of Senegal and the coastal areas; cobalt from Zaire; South African and Mozambiquan chromium; copper from the Shaba and Zambia; uranium from Zaire, Cameroon and Central Africa; vanadium and cadmium from Southwest Africa; bauxite from Guinea and Ghana; on and on. All of these nonferrous ores would in a first stage be exchanged for establishing factories

of various kinds, for machinery and for machine tools with a view to later industrialization.

To the above must also be added the seed oils of all of Africa (especially Senegal), the phosphates of Senegal and Mali, the hevea of the forested regions, cacao, coffee, sugar cane, tea, bananas and other tropical fruits, such as cola nuts; finally, the ironbearing ores themselves of Guinea, Sierra Leone, Mauritania and elsewhere.

A systematic survey of the continent, and Mali in particular, should yield a definitive list of the treasures to be mined, so that once and for all we might get a picture of what industrialization could be like.

4. In the last analysis, the most important investment is of a human character; it is the collective will of the peoples to serve their countries. The establishment of a collective public manpower pool is possible only if none feels frustrated. Before that can be achieved, it would be necessary that, through judicious paring, salaries paid for political positions be brought down to the range of workers' wages.

5. Loans could then be made against international investment funds, but they must never get so high as to risk becoming a delusion. Before everything else, we must help ourselves. What is termed "aid to the underdeveloped countries" might for a long time be used all too easily as blackmail.

There are certain American industrialists who try to prevail on their government to aid only those underdeveloped countries that agree to limit their own emergence. At all times, we would have to be ready to refuse any aid that carried strings with it, however unbinding these might appear to be.

Africa must win and hold in a large part its own domestic market, one of the greatest in the world. A whole book should be devoted to the study of this market with a view to organizing the economies of the African states.

Scientific Research

Basic research will always remain essentially a university concern. Therefore, right at the start, with full objectivity, the university will be rightfully entitled to claim the required funds for the construction of high-energy accelerators, for example, to contribute to the further elucidation of elemental particles, behavior of matter at high levels of energy and other such problems. Applied research must be shared as quickly as possible with specialized institutes under university supervision.

If we wish to see the African Nation everyone is talking about these days adapt itself to the needs of the modern technical world, we have from its very beginnings to provide those technical institutions that guarantee the life of a modern nation. We should forthwith create the following institutes:

A) an institute of nuclear chemistry and physics, to be split in two later, if need be;

B) an electronics institute;

C) an aeronautics and astronautics institute;

D) an institute of applied chemistry for industry and agriculture (organic synthesis, metallurgy, mineral chemical industry and so on);

E) an institute of tropical agronomy and biochemistry (soil study, fertilizers, extraction of vegetable products with a view to finding industrial or pharmaceutical applications for certain flora);

F) an institute of health, specialized in the study of tropical diseases.

The University of Dakar would thus become one of the main training centers for African key personnel.[1]

[1]A few tentative starts have been made toward this end: a University Institute of Technology at Dakar, the Polytechnic Institute at Thiès.

Comparative Production Figures

- Production of electrical energy in the United States (in 1975) was approximately 2,000 billion kilowatt-hours in contrast to that of the USSR, 1,038 billion kWh.
- Worldwide steel production (1974) was estimated at 705 million metric tons, of which 132 million were produced in the United States alone.
- In order to build and put into operation a steelworks complete with rolling mills with a capacity of 4 to 5 million metric tons per year, an African country would have to invest 8 to 10 billion French francs (as of 1974), or approximately $1.6 billion to $2 billion.
- French governmental foreign aid to the French-speaking states of Black Africa and the Indian Ocean in 1977 was estimated at 2.67 billion francs (or approximately $530 million).

A Federated Black Africa has the potential to become both industrially and politically as powerful as either the USSR or the United States.

14 Steps to African Unity

In conclusion, we can specify the following fifteen essential points as basic principles for concrete action:

1. To restore consciousness of our historic unity.

2. To work for linguistic unification on a territorial and continental scale, with a single African cultural and governmental language superseding all others; the European languages, then, whichever they may be, would remain in use or be relegated to the status of foreign languages taught in secondary schools.

3. To raise our national tongues to the rank of governmental languages used in Parliament and in the writing of the laws. Language would no longer stand in the way of electing to Parliament or other office a person from the grass roots who might be unlettered.

4. To work out an *effective* form of representation for the female sector of the nation.

5. To live African federal unity. The immediate unification of French- and English-speaking Africa alone can act as a test for this. It is the only way to start Black Africa along the slope of its historic destiny, once and for all. To wait while invoking secondary considerations is to allow the various states time to harden in their shapes and become unsuited to federation—as in Latin America.

6. To oppose out of hand any idea of creating White states anywhere in Black Africa, no matter where the idea comes from.

7. To make sure our Constitution is so written that no industrial bourgeoisie can come into being. This would prove that we are truly socialist by preventing in advance one of the fundamental ills of capitalism.

Who, today, would oppose a preventive measure of this sort against a class that does not even exist in Africa?

8. To create a powerful State industry, giving primacy to industrialization, development and mechanization of agriculture.

9. To create a powerful modern army, possessing an air force and endowed with a civic education that would make it unlikely to indulge in Latin American-type putsches.

10. To create the technical institutes without which a modern State cannot exist: nuclear physics and chemistry, electronics, aeronautics, applied chemistry and so on.

11. To reduce luxurious living standards and judiciously equalize salaries in such a way that political positions are comparable to workers' jobs.

12. To organize production cooperatives, made up of volunteers owning adjacent fields, in order to mechanize and modernize agriculture and permit large-scale production.

13. To create model State farms with a view to broadening the technical and social experience of still ungrouped individual farmers (peasants). Countryside collectivization will meet with a thousand times less resistance among us than it did in European countries for all of the reasons the author has previously adduced in *L'Afrique noire pré-coloniale* (Pre-Colonial Black Africa).

14. To repopulate Africa in proper time.

15. To carry out with conviction a policy of full employment in order progressively to eliminate the material dependence of certain social categories.[2]

---

[1]It will be noted that these fifteen points were the essential ones of the programs of the BMS (Bloc des masses sénégalaises: Senegalese Masses' Bloc) and the FNS (Front national sénégalais: Senegalese National Front).

Books Consulted

Darnault, Pierre. *Régime de quelques cours d'eau d'Afrique Equatoriale et étude de leur utilisation industrielle.* Paris: Larose, 1947.

Evans, Robley D. *The Atomic Nucleus.* New York: McGraw-Hill Book Co., 1955.

Florio, F. *Cours de Moteurs, Fusées.*

Du Jonchay, Ivan. *Industrialisation de l'Afrique.* Paris: Payot, 1953.

Ioffe, E. *Les semi-conducteurs et leurs applications.* Moscow: Foreign Language Editions, 1957.

Levian. *Aménagement hydraulique.* Paris: Dunod.

Morice, E., & Chartier. *Méthode statistique, 2ème partie. Analyse statistique I.N.S.E.* Paris: Imprimerie Nationale, 1954.

Motte, M.R., Ingénieur E.S.M.E. *Les Transistors.* Paris: Editions Techniques Professionnelles.

Appendix

Interview with Cheikh Anta Diop
by Carlos Moore

Professor Diop was persuaded to break a 15-year silence to speak to Africa and the world, when he was convinced that Afriscope *is a highly serious-minded and uncompromisingly African organ.*

1: Africa's Political Unity

AFRISCOPE: Since the early 1960's the African Continent has shown itself to be coup prone. How do you account for the growing political instability of African regimes?

DIOP: I had foreseen the 'South-Americanization' of the African continent and in my work, *Les Fondaments culturels, techniques et industriels d'un future etat federal d'Afrique noire* (Presence Africaine, 1960), I alluded to this phenomenon. Earlier, in 1956, I also touched on the subject in an article "Alerta sous les tropiques" (*Presence Africaine*, No. 5, Jan. 1956), warning that unless we took care the African continent upon independence would go down the road of 'South-Americanization.' No matter how much one may claim that history doesn't repeat itself, I have nonetheless been haunted by Simon Bolivar's failure to unite the South American continent in a single bloc. It can no longer be denied that Africa is the victim of 'South-Americanization.' That Africa is 'politically unstable' is a fact. We can't even talk anymore about 'balkanization' since

the Balkan regimes are stable, whereas in Africa we have a
change of regime almost every week or every month. At
any rate, every year. And this instability is growing. . . .

In my opinion, what has been lacking are national leaderships which could set an example. Had this been the case,
military overthrows would have been made much more
difficult. At any rate, stability in Africa would have been
much greater. Political selfishness is killing Africa; it's the
basis of the problem. Once African interests become merely
a pretext for individual selfishness, instability necessarily
rears its head. When the only organized force in the country—the army—ceases to respect the civilians in power, it
will seize power for itself.

AFRISCOPE: However, practically each time the army
has seized power, it has perpetrated the same evils it pre-
tended to overthrow. In turn, there is still another coup.

DIOP: Yes, this is true because the army has not in the
meanwhile been educated along patriotic and political lines.
What generally happens is that the army wakes up one day
and discovers that it is merely an instrument of civilians
wielding power. Yet, the army also knows that the survival
of civilian rule depends on army-backing. The contradiction
is solved by a seizure of power. But when the army overthrows civilian rule, without having had any political formation, and when this very army is itself devoid of any
profound ideals, the result of army rule cannot be any
better than the civilian rule it overthrew. . . .

AFRISCOPE: The Economic Community of West African
States (ECOWAS) is the latest regional attempt at regroupment in black Africa. We have seen at least four other such
attempts fail in the past, including the East African Community. Why have all of these projects failed? What chances
do you give ECOWAS?

DIOP: Once again we're putting the cart before the horse.
We want to create regional economic organizations from

which member states can draw maximum benefits, yet we refuse to relinquish even an inch of our respective national sovereignties. There is a serious contradiction here. My opinion is that all such regroupments are bound to fail. In the past, each attempt at regional economic regroupment was shortlived. The reason they have failed and will continue to fail is simple: the links uniting the parties to all such regional agreements have never been irrevocably binding; *nor have the terms of economic cooperation ever been indissoluble.* Moreover, all such attempts at economic regional regroupment have lacked an important and indispensable counterpart: *a supra-national political umbrella, in the sense of an executive organism, able to take political decisions that are binding to all parties.* Consequently, whenever and for whatever reasons one of the parties to the agreement decides to withdraw, the regional grouping starts crumbling. In the absence of a supra-national executive body with full powers, what can prevent a state from pulling out of a regional grouping? In the absence of *irrevocable* commitments, quite naturally involving the partial loss of national sovereignty, what can prevent the party to a regional agreement from withdrawing on a mere whim? . . .

To overcome the tremendous obstacles in the way of the economic unification of Africa, decisive political actions are required in the first place. Political unification is a prerequisite. *The rational organization of African economies cannot precede the political* organization of Africa. The elaboration of a rational formula of economic organization must come *after* the creation of a federal political entity. It is only within the framework of such a geo-political entity that a rational economic development and cooperation can be inserted. The inverse leads to the type of results we have witnessed over the years. If, for example, West Africans had the courage of creating a federal political executive entity with full decision powers, and to which West African states would renounce a definite portion of their national sovereignty, then that would be another matter. In that case, the federal executive body could be asked to draw up carefully studied plans for a rational organization of West African economy. The full powers attributed to such an executive body would allow it to take consequential decisions without fearing that the day after one or another head of state would announce: 'I don't like what's happening; I'm leaving.' It's a vicious circle and we must have the courage to face that fact.

AFRISCOPE: How to break out of this vicious circle?

DIOP: In my opinion, the way out of the present deadlock is quite clear. The rational, economic organization of the African continent or any part of it cannot precede a common political organization along regional or continental federal lines. The first step would be to politically organize a geographic entity and, then, within that geographic space proceed to a rational economic organization. The inverse is not possible. Yet, this is what African heads of state have been trying to do from the very beginning. Why? Simply out of selfishness, out of personal and egoistic power interests. Where does Africa stand in all of this? Selfish African heads of State want to reduce continental and regional exigencies to their own personal and national egoisms. In other words, they latch onto power, have no intention of abandoning it and they talk about creating regional economic interests. However, the defence of power interests is in direct opposition to the avowed wish for regional economic cooperation and unity. It just isn't true that Africa is uppermost in the minds of these heads of state. It is not in the interests of Africa to latch onto power and monopolize it to the extent of refusing to relinquish even a portion of it to a supra-national executive body so as to be able to arrive at an economic union. No one wants to relinquish an iota of national power. That's why all previous regional associations have failed. There's a long list of these and the list is getting even longer. My most sincere wish is that ECOWAS would reverse the trend. But I have no illusions about it. ECOWAS lacks the essential, the one element conditioning its success or failure.

AFRISCOPE: E. Wilmot Blyden in the 1850's, Marcus Garvey in the 1920's and Kwame Nkrumah in the 1960's championed the project of a continental state of Africa. For two decades you have championed the idea yourself. Why, in your opinion, has no African leader taken concrete and decisive steps towards its realization?

DIOP: Whether an African leader has or has not taken concrete steps towards the implementation of this goal, the fact remains that a continental federation is an urgently vital necessity for the totality of African peoples. In my opinion, it is the pre-condition for our collective survival. The more time goes by, the more it will be seen that we must either join in a continental federation or fall into a generalized and endemic state of anarchy. In fact, we have already arrived at that stage . . .

AFRISCOPE: What other concrete instruments of federal control do you propose for a continental union?

DIOP: The links between a federation of African states should be flexible enough to allow each one breathing space. Each national grouping must be left to enjoy the largest possible internal autonomy. But political and economic life must be rationalized from a federal perspective. A certain number of federal agencies must be created; defence, external trade and foreign affairs must definitely be unified. We need a modern continental army worthy of the name, capable of facing any eventuality, rather than our present armies which are mere auxiliaries to the police force. In fact, our armies were not created with the intent of facing up to any external threat. . . .

Whereas there would be administrative autonomy of each member state, the Federal umbrella government would be fully in charge of such activities that go beyond the national prerogatives. For instance, in terms of defence, the armed forces would be on a continental basis. The individual states would have a territorial guard. Troops would be based in various African countries, whether Tanzania, Gabon, Algeria or Libya, and officers would equally come from all regions of the continent. That is, officers and troops based in a state would not necessarily be indigenous to that particular country. Along the same lines, federal administrative cadres would be drawn from all areas of the continent and would serve wherever posted. Continental citizenship is a must. No African should need anymore than an I.D. card for travelling to and from any part of the continent.

A federal African state would have to rationalize African economies on a continental basis. External trade would necessarily fall under the attributions of such a state. The general integration of African economy would allow for the global bargaining of all of Africa's commerciable surplus of raw materials at prices advantageous to us, besides providing a very important source of capital accumulation. The development of our countries, the accelerated formation of technological cadres, as well as the transferral of advanced technology become possible in this context through a rationalization of our commerciable surplus on a continental basis. Naturally, whatever is indispensable to the internal functioning of national economies can be left in the hands of local governments after careful study. As you see, the viability of such a state is certain. In fact, it is the prerequisite for the survival of African peoples. It's the only way out for our countries.

AFRISCOPE: In practical terms, how in your opinion does one go about creating such a state?

DIOP: To begin with a group of states could already band together in an open federation and actively incite the other states to join. I understand that this is more easily said than done, but a start has to be made somehow, somewhere. I see no other way for such a state than in one, two or three·states taking the initiative of surrendering a good part of their own national sovereignty and accepting to be the initial nucleus of an open federation. This demands courage, a lot of courage, political foresight and, above all, a deep profound commitment to Africa as a historical, cultural, and political entity.

AFRISCOPE: How would the wielding of political power be organized?

DIOP: A collegial system of political leadership could be envisaged, based on the concept of rotation. For instance, an executive council of the federated states, comprised of the heads of those states could be set up. The federated states would have to accept a permanent, *irrevocable* transfer of part of their national sovereignty to such an executive council. That is, from the outset, the nucleus of federated states would integrate their defence, economy, external trade, civil service and foreign affairs. These would be prerogatives of the federal executive council. Equally, universities and scientific research centres would be unified and rationalized on a federal basis. The president of such a federation could be elected from within the federal executive council itself. That system could be adopted at a first stage, since continental-wide elections presuppose the existence of a continental federation. In as much as the functions of a federal president would be symbolized by a person, such a person could be one of the heads of the federated states. Leadership, however, would be exercised on a collegial basis. Also, the presidency of the federal executive council would be on a rotative basis. Every two, four, or seven years, or whatever the case may be, the

presidency would go to one of the heads of the federated
states. We need some kind of convenient formula that would
ensure stability. In fact, we could even envision a rotative
system based on alphabetical order. This would eliminate
the type of rivalries that could jeopardize the stable functioning of such a federal state. The important thing is that
the federal executive council be a truly democratic and
collegial body, open to discussions and thorough analyses of
each and every problem that might affect Africa as a whole.
However, once decisions have been' democratically arrived
at by consensus, all federated states should be bound to
them. In synthesis, I am in favour of any sort of formula
that would allow African peoples and countries to bind
together democratically in defence of their common interests and that would ensure their own survival. . . .

AFRISCOPE: On the informal plane, what measures
would you suggest for arousing a continental African consciousness?

DIOP: We could go and on. . . . But a practical thing leading to a continental consciousness is inter-African contacts
on an informal free and leisurely basis. An aspect of the
problem of the unification of the African continent, and
which is seldom stressed, deals with an inter-African tour-
ist circuit. A special agency must be created for this pur-
pose. Africans do not know Africa. How can you love a
country, or have faith in its destiny, if you don't know it? All
the more, how can we love our continent or develop a
continental consciousness without knowing it?. . . .

2: Obstacles to Emancipation and Unity

AFRISCOPE: The western bloc is setting up South Africa
as a permanent white bastion-state enclaved in Africa. The
'bantustan' policy and so-called 'independence' of Transkei

are the corollaries to this plot. Isn't the existence of a white South Africa a monumental obstacle in the way of a continental African state?

DIOP: Without a shadow of a doubt. The setting up of a continental African state presupposes the eradication of the South African threat. The establishment of a white state anywhere on the continent of Africa is inconceivable, inadmissible. The whites who are in southern Africa could remain there, but only within the framework of black majority rule. A borderline between a white state and a black state is inconceivable. Sooner or later it will lead to a racial war. . . . The white South African regime is a permanent danger which should act as a mobilizing force for all Africans. We should have no illusions about this. It is either unity or destruction!

AFRISCOPE: With the active complicity of the West, fascist South Africa is developing its nuclear capability at an alarming speed. This poses the threat of extermination of black peoples. Yet, some African leaders insist that dialogue is the only way of averting that danger.

DIOP: Nothing could be more dangerous than to initiate dialogue with white South Africa. It would merely give her the necessary time to put the finishing touches on her nuclear program. South Africa only believes in one solution and speaks only one language: brute force. Look at Soweto! To the white fascist leaders of South Africa, any black country is Soweto. South Africa is feverishly preparing for a showdown. Pretoria now knows that *any technically organized minority, fully equipped and enjoying a high educational standard can successfully face and repulse by violent means an entire continent which has remained at the level of semi-development.* South Africa is actively working to achieve an equilibrium of terror. Pretoria is going about acquiring the most sophisticated and efficient nuclear weapons, along with the vectors to deliver them to any point on the African continent.

South Africa is virtually a nuclear power and is preparing to put up a long and terrible resistance to the rest of the continent. Objectively speaking, South Africa does not consider anyone on the African continent as her 'friend.' What we have are these so-called pacifists who are trying to camouflage their cowardice and capitulation by proposing a so-called dialogue with a regime that has vowed to destroy the black man. The policy of dialogue with South Africa, presented to us as the product of political 'realism' can only be judged as political blindness or the surrender of the best interests of African peoples. It takes two to dialogue. South Africa is not seeking dialogue but time; the necessary time to develop her nuclear arsenal. I don't think any African leader ignores this, though some pretend to.

Whereas it was previously believed that Pretoria would fabricate nuclear weapons by 1983, the latest developments force us to drastically revise that prediction. South Africa is now in the position to become a full nuclear power within the next few years at maximum. *If only for this reason, the struggle for the overthrow of white supremacist South Africa must be intensified immediately!* No compromise! No procrastination! The armed struggle in southern Africa must be intensified immediately! It's the only way to avert a nuclear war in Africa in the near future. Once South Africa acquires nuclear weapons, it will be too late. At that time, the African states which are today invoking 'realism' to justify their inaction and capitulation in face of Pretoria will definitely have a good argument to preach permanent peaceful coexistence with the white South African regime. However, what they might not realize is that once South Africa acquires nuclear weapons, a *modus vivendi* will be impossible, no matter how much African states bend over. *Once South Africa acquires nuclear weapons, she will take the offensive. Therein lies the reason why a borderline between a white and black state is impossible on the Af-*

rican continent. It signified war sooner or later. South Africa knows it and is preparing for it. . . .

It is irrational to think that any African, wherever he may be, can make plans for the future as long as the South African threat is not eradicated. South Africa is the stumbling block in the way of African development. In fact, it has become imperative to liberate South Africa in time so as to avert a nuclear war. To wait is to allow South Africa the time to leisurely develop its nuclear capability. If this is allowed, there will be an equilibrium of terror whereby the other African states will be impotent to act. *So, in the interests of world peace itself, we must immediately intensify the struggle for the liberation of southern Africa.* Otherwise, whatever political or other projects we might conceive will be devoid of any meaning. The racist regime of South Africa must be liquidated without delay. *Otherwise, there will be an atomic war in Africa in the next five to ten years.* Already, within less than six years from now, South Africa will dispose of a small stockpile of nuclear weapons; quite enough to create mass panic among Africans. . . .

AFRISCOPE: Technologically speaking, at what stage of development can South Africa's nuclear capability be assessed now?

DIOP: With the complicity of the West, South Africa has been able to come up with an absolutely revolutionary and efficient method for the separation of isotopes. . . . When first announced, it was believed Pretoria was bluffing. It was no bluff at all! At Velindaba there is a pilot centre where South Africa has been able to experiment with this new method of isotopic separation. She was helped by the German firm, Steag. That centre is now fully operational and can allow Pretoria to assemble the most difficult of atomic bombs; that is, the Uranium-235 bomb. Moreover, South Africa definitely has the know-how of reprocessing spent nuclear reactor fuel (uranium fuel). She can therefore manufacture plutonium atomic bombs. [Spent uranium is the waste from a nuclear power reactor, that when processed through a special reprocessing plant, creates plutonium. It takes about 13 pounds of plutonium to make a small atomic bomb.—Ed.]. Thus, with her present nuclear installation, South Africa can build atomic bombs based on plutonium-239. Furthermore, she will be able to go directly into the U-235 category. This is extremely serious, for unless science comes up with another shortcut, the U-235 bomb is indispensable as a *trigger* for a thermonuclear bomb. What all of this means is that South Africa is not only in possession of advanced nuclear technology, and on the verge of building classical plutonium atomic bombs, but more importantly, very close to the thermonuclear stage!

Right now, South Africa has what we can call a *nuclear capability.* I don't believe she will wait another five, six or ten years to build atomic weapons, considering the mounting political pressures she faces from black Africa. At present, she would have to enlarge the pilot installation she already has, discreetly improve it and make it run day and night to isolate enough U-235 to build the type of bomb acquirable *without* a nuclear plant. It's quite possible that Pretoria already has the data whereby she could manufacture an atomic bomb without the need for a nuclear plant. Needless to say, whenever South Africa does acquire a nuclear plant, her production of fissionable material will have been multiplied by one hundred. Whereas she may now be able to build one or two bombs, with a nuclear plant she will be turning out one hundred bombs instead. There's no doubt about that. The danger is staring us in the eyes. In fact, the situation will be untenable whenever her nuclear plants become operational.

AFRISCOPE: South Africa invaded Angola in 1975. Israel attacked Uganda in 1976. Israel and South Africa are allies; they are both virtual nuclear powers. Shouldn't we read in their actions against Africa an ominous sign of things to come?

DIOP: Concerning South Africa, the dangers are real; there's no question about it. The connivance between South Africa and Israel is really astonishing. One would have thought that a people such as the Israelis, who had suffered from racism in modern times, would have aligned themselves with black people, the veritable historical victims of racism. To my great surprise I realised that something essential was missing in the relationship between black and Israeli peoples. We have seen Israel choose the western camp. Yet, the recent past of the Israeli people would have justified the expectance of their aligning themselves with those who have also suffered as the Israelis, if not more, from the ravages of racism. In other words, we would have expected Israel to have sided with black peoples particularly and the Third World in general. We would have expected a non-expansionist attitude on the part of Israel, which is not the case. We would have expected understanding on the part of Israel, which is not the case. We would have expected sympathy from the Israelis for the cause of the Third World in general, which is not the case. Instead, Israel chose the western camp. . . .

AFRISCOPE: After Vorster's visit to Israel, are we not to fear that Tel Aviv will help Pretoria develop its nuclear weapons?

DIOP: The Israeli-South African alliance defies the imagination! Against all expectations, Israel has done the unimaginable. From this point on, anything can be expected. We know Israel to be in possession of a small stockpile of operational nuclear weapons and to be a highly advanced technological nation. We're now justified in believing that Israel will put her advanced nuclear technology at the disposal of the fascist South African regime, enabling it to skip the stages in the obtaining of operational nuclear weapons. More specifically, Israel is in the position to help South Africa develop the triggering device for her nuclear weapons. In fact, with Israeli aid, South African atomic scientists and engineers will be able to considerably cut down the period normally necessary for achieving operational nuclear devices. This new alarming development is to be feared. South Africa has the raw materials, advanced technology and the material means to become a nuclear power in a very short period of time. With Israeli aid, that period of time will be even shorter. Moreover, once Pretoria will have received the nuclear plants recently negotiated with France, she will be able to multiply by 100 her nuclear capacity production. As I've said before, I fear South Africa will manufacture nuclear weapons in a record time, thus surprising the entire African continent. Once this becomes a *fait accompli*, the struggle against South Africa will have acquired entirely new and foreboding consequences.

AFRISCOPE: Once South Africa is ready to take the offensive, no doubt using nuclear weapons, isn't it conceivable that Israel would equally join Pretoria in a two-pronged assault against the black continent?

DIOP: South Africa, no doubt, wouldn't hestitate to commit nuclear genocide on the black peoples of Africa. In fact, it's certain that such a plan is in the back of the minds of the white supremacist leaders of that black country. Could we foresee the possibility that Israel, from the Middle East, and South Africa, from the southern tip of the continent, would combine their forces to launch a nuclear attack on black Africa with the aim of exterminating its peoples? An answer to that question is, perforce, hazardous. . . . Yet, in view of recent events, we must pay the most serious attention to strategic possibilities of that nature. . . .

AFRISCOPE: Do you think that Israel's position in the Middle East vis-à-vis Arabs is analogous to the position of white South Africa in respect of Africans?

DIOP: Within the Arab world the state of Israel finds itself in an entirely different context. My opinion is that whether one likes it or not, the state of Israel will in the long run be absorbed by the Arab world. True, there is a technological gap between both at present. As long as a portion of the Arab world remains at a nomadic stage, Israeli technology will of course make itself felt. In that context, Israel will continue to appear as a western prolongation in the Middle East. However, Middle Eastern Arab countries will develop technologically, closing the present gap. The state of Israel will then be completely absorbed demographically by the Arab World. Therefore, in the long run, the Arab-Israeli conflict will abate. In fact, if the state of Israel would right now desist from its bellicose attitude and would seek a viable *modus vivendi* with her Arab neighbors, Arab-Israeli peace would come about very quickly. My opinion is that the Arab-Israeli conflict will necessarily evolve in the direction of a peaceful solution acceptable to both parties. This is all the more likely given the historical context underlying the relationship of these two Semitic peoples.

I foresee a time in the near future when the Arab and Israeli ethnic groups, which have a very old common historical past in the Middle East, will peacefully resolve their differences. Both peoples belong to the same Semitic branch. The defeat of Israel can already be determined by the geographic context of the Middle East. Israel finds herself too isolated in that region not to ultimately seek a peaceful solution. Arab and Israeli cultures are very close to one another. Such affinities extend into the realm of religion. As we know, the Muslim and Judaic religions emerged from a common source, from practially a common people and from the same geographical area. Eventually, both Semitic groups will again fuse. None of the foregoing considerations apply to South Africa in regards to the rest of Africa.

AFRISCOPE: The aim of Pan-Arabism, as defined by Gamal Abdul Nasser, is the formation of a federation of North African and Asian Arab states as a single political and economic entity. Doesn't that project conflict with that of a federal continental African state?

DIOP: The way I see it is that there already exists a continental African consciousness. For lack of a precise Pan-African project, however, certain North African Arab countries might be tempted to group separately with Asian Arabs. In face of the disunity and uncertainty characteristic of intra-African politics, North African Arab states might indeed be instinctively tempted to seek fusion with their Middle Eastern brethren. Nevertheless, I believe that a continent-wide African consciousness does exist already. When you go to North Africa, to Algeria, Morocco, Egypt, for example, you can detect an African *behaviour.* We can build on this as long as an effort is made to forget many painful things of the past. Africans to the north and south of the continent must think in terms of uniting because it is in their global interests to do so. If we can overcome prejudices and fears through information and open discussion, then the advantages of a continental federal state are apparent. We might nuance our opinion on the steps to be taken towards establishing such a state. To begin with, there could be a federation of the Maghreb (Morocco, Algeria, Tunisia, Libya, Egypt) on the one hand, while on the other, a federation of all the sub-Saharan African countries. A confederation of these two federations could then be envisioned. With time, both entities could fuse so as to arrive at a true continental federal state. This is possible. Hence, the North and the South could be federated independently, then subsequently fused. A lot of effort would have to be expended in destroying prejudices, fears and susceptibilities and creating the basis for a common understanding between North African Arabs and sub-Saharan Africans.

AFRISCOPE: Nevertheless, Arab countries are increasingly forming exclusive organizations of all kinds from which sub-Saharan African states are excluded but which include Asian and North African Arabs. In fact, there are no less than 25 such organizations. The most recently formed are ALECSO (an exclusively Arab Unesco) and CASTARAB (or standing Arab Scientific Conference). Besides, isn't there a discrepancy in North African Arab states being members simultaneously of the Arab League and the O.A.U.?

DIOP: I won't deny that there are great difficulties in bringing Arab North Africa and sub-Saharan Africa together in a federal continental political union. Difficulties do exist. I still continue to believe, however, that an African continental state is vital to the survival of all Africans, to the North and South of the Sahara. Ways and means must be found to overcome the obstacles in its path. . . .

AFRISCOPE: Supposing the assumption of a common historical destiny between North African and Asian Arabs proves stronger than the pan-African common interests you speak of?

DIOP: If despite goodwill on our part, North African Arabs were to refuse a continental federation, then nothing should stand in the way of the formation of an exclusively sub-Saharan continental federation. However, I feel that if the perspective of a continental federation were clearly defined, backed by a strong sub-Saharan wish in this direction, then North African states would have to reconsider their position on that score, when if prior to that they were thinking along other lines. Should this not be the case, then black Africa couldn't be blamed in the future for grouping along purely sub-Saharan lines. The fault would not be

ours. Nevertheless, I think we must push the experience to
its logical conclusions. . . .

AFRISCOPE: Gamal Abdul Nasser's project was that of
an "Arab Nation" from the Nile to the Euphrates. Egypt
tried to federate with Syria and northern Yemen. Libya has
now taken up the project.

DIOP: The very failure of the Egypt/Syria federation
shows how difficult it is for African states to look outside of
Africa for a federation. In fact, that failure should be a
warning; a political federation involving states situated in
Africa cannot be extra-African. Nothing prevents North
African Arab states, within the context of a continental
African state, to maintain cultural contacts with Arabs of
Asia, with whom they share a common language. Again, it
would be as if black Africans were prevented from establishing close cultural links with blacks of the Americas and
the rest of the black world. One thing is to establish cultural
ties and another to form a *political* federation. This is
absolutely clear. Our objectives must be the creation of an
economic and politically federated continent. All Africans
who express the desire to build such a federation, irrespective of whether they be from the North or sub-Saharan
Africa, must be welcomed on an equal footing. I am convinced that if vigorous propaganda were made in this sense,
we would end up with very positive results. . . .

AFRISCOPE: However, Col. Muammar Qaddafi of Libya
and others still agitate along these lines.

DIOP: People must have entire freedom to talk and ex-
pound their views even when these ideas are not realizable.
My opinion is that too many divergencies exist for such a
project to materialize. The concept of an Arab state from
the Atlantic to the Persian Gulf is devoid of any economic
base, whereas I can very well conceive of North African
Arab states joining the rest of Africa to form a viable
political economic entity. As I said, membership in such a

continental political arrangement should not prevent North African Arabs from continuing to entertain close cultural links with the Arabs of Asia. By the same token, a continental political federation including North African Arabs should in no way prevent black Africans from entertaining the closest cultural links with blacks of the Americas, Oceania and Asia. It is absolutely indispensable to make the difference between relationships based on a cultural continuum and those based on a geo-political entity. . . .

AFRISCOPE: Suppose Asian and North African Arabs short-circuited black Africa and agreed to set up what Qaddafi has been agitating for.

DIOP: If that was ever to be the case, then, it would be explicitly clear that a federation with black Africa was being rejected. If we black Africans take steps to include North African Arabs into a continental federation and the latter prefer instead to elaborate organic political ties with Arabs of Asia, this would be tantamount to a rebuff. If north African states, rather than looking to black Africa in a natural partnership, preferred a federation with Asian Arabs extending to the Persian Gulf, *then we would be entirely justified to organize ourselves in an exclusively sub-Saharan federation.* In such an eventuality, no one could accuse sub-Saharan Africans of being guilty of exclusivism, since their appeals to the North would have been refused. However, I do not really envision this being the case. Rather, my feeling is that the necessary ideological and propaganda work in favour of an all inclusive continental federation has to be undertaken as of now.

AFRISCOPE: Many Africans argue that the very cohesion of the Arabs as an ethno-cultural entity would pose the problem of their dominating any confederal arrangement.

DIOP: Sub-Saharan Africans must realize that they have nothing to lose culturally, politically or otherwise in a federation which includes Arab North Africa. Black Africa would not be an appendage of the Arab world in such a federation. There is a distinct African identity which can and ought to be continually developed. In the past 20 years a lot of work has been done in terms of reinforcing the cultural, linguistic and historical identity of African peoples. The black world has reinforced its cultural personality. As a consequence of this development, our cultural, linguistic and historical personality can no longer be strangled in any way by cultural contacts with other peoples. The time has come for us to abandon our complexes and work in favour of a union that is favourable to all Africans. That's the crux of the matter.

In the final analysis, what is really at the core of the controversy of whether North and sub-Saharan Africans can join in a common federation is the question: Are we culturally ready to meet with the Arab world? Are we culturally ready to join in a common federation without surrendering an inch of our cultural, linguistic and historical identity as black Africans? This is the real question. My answer is affirmative. Black Africa has recovered its cultural personality to an extent and vigour which makes it impossible for anyone to strangle it. What remains to be done is the day-to-day work of solidifying and redefining in all areas the contours of this distinct personality. Considering all of the efforts which have been accomplished in sub-Saharan Africa in terms of the restoration of our historical and cultural identity, Africans no longer have to fear being dominated by the Arabs. . . .

AFRISCOPE: Don't you think that another serious stumbling block in the way of the constitution of a continental state would appear to be the entrenchment of staunchly egoistic neocolonial regimes both in North and sub-Saharan Africa?

DIOP: Definitely. It's obvious that once we eliminate difficulties of a subjective nature—that is, whether North and sub-Saharan Africans do or do not want to federate—there remain the objective obstacles of a political nature. The egoistic nature of certain political regimes, north and south of the Sahara, is such that they are terrified at the idea of a continental African state. The stranglehold of alien economic interests is not foreign to that fear. The neocolonial character of such regimes is therefore an objective factor in the way of constituting a continental federation.

African unity, I feel, will come from the base and develop as an undercurrent to the present political sterility and economic stagnancy rampant on our continent. A feeling of general insecurity, generated by the ineptitude of African regimes in dealing with the most crucial issues—including that of South Africa—will result in the masses entering the picture sooner or later. . . . As generalized insecurity spreads, no African regime will be able to prevent the masses from seeing that the ineptitude of their own governments is linked to this general insecurity. At that point, I feel the masses will find within their own ranks the type of political vanguards, made up of young, altruistic and politically motivated Africans, to unleash a powerful continent-wide movement. This political undercurrent would eventually be forced to sweep away the objective obstacles standing in the way of a continental African federation.

AFRISCOPE: Ideological bloc bi-polarity seems to be installing itself in African politics. What ideological preference, in your view, would the united foreign policy of a continental African state reflect?

DIOP: A continental African state must, of necessity, be non-aligned. Africa then will be a continent *with its own specific political personality.* In time, Africa would have to play a world role. *A continental African state must be an end in itself!* It would even be humiliating to conceive of a

continental African state being towed as a vessel by any
other state, government or bloc. A continental African
state would entertain relations with all other countries on a
perfectly equal footing. How else could Africa lift itself to
the level of the other powerful states and deal with the rest
of the world from a position of true independence?

Today, only three states can be considered as independent: the United States, the Soviet Union, China. These
three states are organized on a continental basis. That's no
accident. Significantly, Europe is now trying desperately to
federate itself into one continental state. Highly industrial
and technological European states are trying to elect a pan-
European parliament, establish an economic common market, attempting to unify their defence and foreign policies
and preaching in favour of the continental federal approach!
That's an edifying example for us Africans. I'm even hoping
that the European states succeed and thus show the way to
Africa, considering that African leaderships tend to ape
European initiatives. Since Africa is so prone to imitating
Europe for the better or the worse, that's one initiative we
can start imitating as of now. For once it would be a positive
imitation! Even Europe is showing the way and attesting to
the fact that the 19th century mini-states have become an
anachronism in our epoch. A great political future is in
store for Europe because all European problems are being
seen by European leaderships as *continental* European
problems. Why is it any different for Africa? Why should
the underdeveloped mini-states be valid for Africa when
the super-developed mini-states are invalid for Europe?
Only the blindest form of selfishness could restrict the
vision of African leaderships to the confines of their mini-
states. Even a lucid selfishness would dictate that *the conti-*
nental solution is the only one. Only this can prevent the
voice of Africa from merely being an echo of some other
state or block.

3: Culture, Negritude, and the African Personality

AFRISCOPE: What is the actual mission of culture?
DIOP: Survival and creativity. Man must create to survive. To create he must ensure his survival.

Collective historical consciousness is one of man's chief means of survival and a source of creation. Destroy or stifle it and the chances for the survival of a people become questionable. The cultural personality of Africa is inseparable from the restoration of our collective historical consciousness. Because most people are vaguely conscious of their local historical past they end up flirting with their own past. Most of us are not even equipped to systematically refer to the Nile Valley for an understanding of either the present-day or ancient structures of our societies. Yet, we can make very little headway in understanding our cultures, languages and social structures without a thorough knowledge of the many facets of ancient Egyptian civilization. Ancient black Egypt was in every sense the actual cradle of our cultures.

Without a systematic reference to Egypt, there can be no true cultural renaissance in Africa. Afterall, what is our objective if it is not that of recovering and promoting the *creativity* of our peoples? Man's mission is *creation*. African renaissance, black renaissance, is inseparable from the restoration of the black world's creativity.

To assume his destiny, man must be a creator irrespective of his race. The loss of our national sovereignty strangled our independent creativity. Today, as black people are slowly recovering their national sovereignty, we are obliged to free ourselves from all forms of cultural alienation. Without that internal recovery and psychic self-appraisal, very little can be accomplished. The recovery of political sovereignty is merely one aspect of the question. Economic sovereignty is another. Psychic autonomy is yet another. All three must combine in a dynamic renovative effort. These are the terms by which I define the African and world black renaissance.

The restoration of the historical consciousness of black and African peoples, with all its implications, necessarily leads to a veritable reversal of perspectives and to a fundamental transformation of our cultural relationship with the rest of the world. Black peoples have been weighed on the scales of history by others and been found wanting.

Yet, once we awaken to the historical realities through a scientific approach to history, we find that the very people who were considered to be historical debtors were actually the historical creditors. From ancient Egypt, from the oldest world civilization, came the scientific and technological knowledge, the religious ideas and cultural, artistic contributions which shaped the earliest cultures of the European world. The day when Africans and blacks in general will impose that point of view, a view supported by scientifically verifiable historical data, the self-image of blacks and the warped image that others entertain about blacks will have to undergo a most profound revision. It will mean that an entire vision of the universe will have to be changed. The hour is therefore approaching when other peoples will have to divest themselves, even against their conscious will, of the falsifications and lies that have buried the original and unique contributions of the black man to world history. To that end we must work, fully equipped with the tools of science in every conceivable discipline. We should never lose sight of the fact that the restoration of the cultural personality of African and black peoples in general can only be achieved through *struggle*.

AFRISCOPE: Many people attack Negritude as a deceptive concept. Others defend it as a philosophy of African and black rehabilitation. You are among its critics. Yet, all of your works deal with the historical, cultural and social rehabilitation of the black man. What, then, is your concept of Negritude?

DIOP: I really wouldn't like to get into that! There are just too many emotional and conflicting issues involved. It would be too long to get into such a complex question. . . .

AFRISCOPE: Precisely, this is why your comments on it are vitually important. It's an important issue.

DIOP: If we want to talk about Negritude, the case of a man like Aime Cesaire must be treated all by itself. Cesaire is an exceptional literary genius. He is undoubtedly one of the greatest creative minds of the black world. He's a man who lives his philosophy. He's a man truly committed to the cause of the black world and to the progress of oppressed mankind. He's an unflinching anticolonialist. Because of this, Cesaire was practically the only one to have played a decisive and personal role in the mobilization of the black students who were in France during the colonial period. He summoned all of us to our feet in the struggle against the colonial oppressors. At political meetings we were all capti-vated by Cesaire, his clear thinking and lucid appraisal of the colonial question. Cesaire was always physically pre-sent at our meetings, alongside all those who were fighting colonialism. In fact, all of us used to talk about Cesaire, his genius, his sincerity and devotion to the black and anti-colonialist struggle. We weren't talking about Negritude. Cesaire was magnetic, vigorous and poetic. Cesaire created the term *Negritude,* and at the time we devoured his works.

Negritude, as it became known, was originally a West Indian creation; Africans confiscated and monopolized it in post-colonial times! During the post-colonial epoch an en-tirely different interpretation was given the term Negritude. Under this blanket term a flood of literature emerged, the content of which was clearly deceptive. In fact, as far as I can remember, the term Negritude was only applied to a literary or political current after Jean Paul Sartre's *Black Orpheus* written in 1948. Cesaire coined the term but prior to the publication of Sartre's book I knew of no political or literary current which went under the name of Negritude. This is an important element. Actually, what was done in the post-colonial epoch was to gather the political anti-colonial black movements and writings of the 1930's and 40's and place them under the blanket term Negritude. This was done only after, and as a consequence of Jean Paul Sartre's theorizations in *Black Orpheus*.

In the 1940's, along with Cesaire, there were men of the caliber of Leon Damas, who was also anti-colonialist. However, Damas' role was smaller than that of Cesaire, who in fact dwarfed everyone else with his intense commitment and action against colonialism. At that time there were other black intellectuals in Paris who were defending the colonial status quo with philosophical arguments. Their writings were indigestible to the mass of black students in Paris at that time. The difficulty today when evoking Negritude resides in the fact that certain people use Cesaire as a cover to fend off attacks from those who consider the post-colonial utilization of Negritude as an obvious imposture. This is why all discussions on Negritude must begin with a separate appraisal of Cesaire, the man, the literary genius, the clairvoyant political agitator and determined anti-colonialist. All of us who knew Cesaire during those years and who have continued to relate to him since then have an immense respect for his work, his integrity and lasting contribution to the emancipation of black people. Cesaire cannot be associated with anything other than the struggle against colonialism and the emancipation of black people. When I talk about Cesaire, I don't talk about Negritude; I talk about Cesaire, the man I knew and respected, the genius, the fighter. Through his actions and works, Cesaire exercised a personal influence on all those who came into contact with him. He continues to do so today over the younger generation.

Cesaire showed where there was a definite cultural alienation among blacks, more pronounced in the West Indies than in Africa, which required special attention in the struggle against colonialism. His aim therefore was to recover the lost cultural personality of colonized black societies. He attempted this through poetry. Hence, he extolled the psychic factor as a necessary component of a new African cultural personality and national consciousness. Let's say he rediscovered, or introduced, the psychic and cultural factor into the struggle of black peoples to regain their national sovereignty usurped by colonialism. Cesaire thus wrote about how the black world lives, feels and suffers. He attached importance to the differential psychology of Africans, blacks, as opposed to Europeans. The poetry of Cesaire, his literary creation, centered on the convulsions of the 'black soul' when subjected to the oppressive conditions of colonialism. Militant action was attached to the new form of poetry among black intellectuals. Cesaire's poetry was definitely not an abstract literary effort but was rooted in the suffering of Africans, blacks. . . . In a famous line of his extremely sensitive, beautiful, violent *Cashier d'un retour au pays natal*, Cesaire wrote:

My negritude is not a rock, its deafness hurled against the clamor of the day.

My negritude is not a film of dead water on the dead eye of the earth.

My negritude is neither a tower nor a cathedral.

It plunges into the red flesh of the earth.

It plunges into the burning flesh of the sky.

It pierces the opaque prostration by its upright patience.

Published in 1947, these lines were the words of a profoundly committed militant. The man who wrote these lines was loved, respected and revered by all those who dreamt of freedom and independence and were working toward that goal. Jacques Rabemananjara of Madagascar, Leon Damas of Guyana, and many others were among them. They all spoke and wrote in moving terms about the 'black soul' and the suffering of black people. There were many West Indians among them. These militant intellectuals, Africans or West Indians, were therefore talking, writing and acting within the context of the anti-colonial struggle. We weren't talking then about Negritude.

AFRISCOPE: In other words, your scientific researches were spurred by the existence of a colonial order and by the cultural and psychic disorders analyzed by Frantz Fanon?

DIOP: That's correct. But that motivation wasn't called Negritude then. When I started writing *Black Nations and Culture,* I approached the problem of black subjugation from a different perspective than the literary anti-colonialist of the 1940's. Not being a poet, nor a literary man, I did not approach it from the psychic angle which had made Cesaire's poetry such an irresistible and cutting weapon in the awakening of an African anti-colonial consciousness. I realized that the cultural personality of a people, of any people, was made up of three interrelated factors. The *psychic* factor. The *linguistic* factor. The *historical* factor. I didn't invent that notion. Others had outlined it before. I merely saw it to be a fact. Hence, my efforts were geared towards the restoration of the *linguistic* and *historical* personality of black Africans. The poets of what was later called Negritude had emphasized the psychic element which is undoubtedly one of the components of the cultural personality of a people. . . .

I understood my scientific researches at a time when the prevalent and accepted data concerning the historical past of black societies was a misleading one. My cultural approach was scientific, rather than poetic. Once on scientific terrain I had only objective phenomena to analyze. I realized that out of the three components of the cultural identity of a people, *only two could be apprehended scientifically, i.e. the linguistic and historical factors.* I therefore laboured towards restoring the historical and linguistic personality of black peoples. I also worked towards the restoration of our common historical past by attaching primordial significance to the oldest and most accomplished civilization elaborated by black African peoples: ancient Egypt! Once I had realized that the collective personality, the cultural identity of a people, centered on three components-linguistic, historical and psychic—I concentrated my scientific efforts along the two lines which could be grasped objectively by scientific research. That has been my approach to the cultural rehabilitation of the black man and of black societies.

AFRISCOPE: The difference, then, in your approach to the rehabilitation of the black man and that of the Negritude poets of the 1940's is in your emphasis on sociology, linguistics, and history?

DIOP: Exactly! By describing the political and social structures inherited from our common historical past, and which reflect the conditions in which our ancestors lived, I was able to make a contribution to our rehabilitation. I was not, however, describing any sort of permanent state in man, since human beings are conditioned by their social and physical environment. Once you change the social environment, even a black man who has been conditioned by a communitarian life-style can become the most individualistic and self-centered being. Consequently, my work in history, sociology and linguistics kept to the path of objective verifiable reality. By throwing light on the falsifications to which the historical past of the black man has been subjected, these historical, sociological, and linguistic studies serve to reinforce the cultural personality of Africans. The cultural renaissance of our people is inconceivable outside of the restoration of both our historical past and our languages to a privileged position as the vehicles of modern education, technology, science, and the creative sensibility of our people.

As long as the historical path linking us to our ancestors is not understood, critically appraised, legitimized, we will be unable to build a new culture. To this end the retrieval of our national languages is foremost.

A systematic policy in favour of their growth, the inclusion of a modern technological and scientific lexicon, can no longer be eluded. The path which leads us to our ancestors and which led our ancestors to us cannot be understood without a systematic reference to ancient Egyptian civilization. In fact, it is impossible to elaborate a new body of social studies without a systematic reference to ancient Egypt. Ancient Egypt plays for Africa and blacks in general the same role which Greco-Latin culture plays for the western world. From the outset, my researches were centred on ancient Egypt, its culture, language, religion, and science. I demonstrated the profound links binding the ancient Egyptians to modern black Africans, not only racially and culturally, but also linguistically.

AFRISCOPE: As a literary current, would you say that Negritude has neglected the objective basis of society in favour of the purely subjective world?

DIOP: That's certainly so in the case of post-colonial 'Negritude'! In fact, I see a total incompatibility between the formal defence of African culture on the one hand, and the systematic refusal on the other to adopt concrete measures to develop our national languages. Those who are incapable of solving this problem can do nothing for African culture. They merely embrace African culture to better smother it. Their attitude shows them to be impostors. Take a country like Senegal, for example, where 95% of the population speaks Wolof. How can one understand the fact that some people are panic-striken when the adoption of Wolof is proposed as the official national language? If the Senegalese people can't be helped to retrieve and develop their linguistic unity *now*, what use is there to talk about defending African culture? In contrast to this, the attitude of someone like Julius Nyerere is consequential. Without rhetorics or fanfare, he elevated Swahili to the status of a national and governmental language.

Flight from one's own language is the quickest shortcut to cultural alienation. For Africa this has been a monumental problem, but it has to be tackled head on. I have attempted to do this in my works and my most thorough contribution on this subject will soon be available *(The Genetic Kinship of Pharonic Egyptian and African Languages)*. Too often we talk about culture without grabbing the cow by the horns, as the saying goes. Why? Simply because we are contented with compromises that avoid the adoption of a radical stance in face of cultural problems. Few of us dare go to the roots of the problem via a scientific approach. As a result, many of those who *talk* about promoting our national languages limit their intent to the domain of folklore. When they want to deal with serious questions, they turn to the languages of . . . Europe!

AFRISCOPE: Kwame Nkrumah had opposed his concept of 'African Personality' to the concept of 'Negritude.' Are both concepts antithetical or do they converge anywhere?

DIOP: They converge in the sense that both deal in generalities! We must get down to the facts, to the objective apprehendable realities. When we talk about personality, meaning the personality of collective groups, we can only mean a *cultural personality.* And what is the basis of the cultural personality of a people, African or otherwise, if not a historical, psychic, and linguistic self-consciousness? These three elements are the constituent elements of a people's cultural personality or identity. They are not static factors, but factors conditioned by humanity's social and physical environment. You have already seen my own approach to the problem of restoring the historical foundations of African cultures through scientific research in the fields of history and linguistics. Moreover, you can also see where that approach has also clarified what is called the particular sensibility of the black person, or 'black soul.' I have tried determining the nature of the black particularity in history and to ascertain the way in which the 'black soul' or 'black sensibility' has influenced the material existence and creativity of black peoples by using the *structures* evolved by ancient black societies as a basis. Consequently, I analyzed family structures, clannic and tribal organization and finally the territorial state. These structures are the objective reflection of precise historical conditions and also of what is called the 'black soul.' So, my approach to the 'black soul' has been through history, linguistics and the material structures of ancient black societies. Rather than deal in generalities, we must know what the 'black soul' is because its *our* soul. The way I saw it at the beginning was that Africa's soul had been 'stolen' and could only be retrieved through a scientific approach.

In synthesis, we cannot oppose 'African Personality' to 'Negritude' since both deal with only one of the three components determining the cultural identity of a people. People *live* their culture. The roots of their culture are inseparable from their linguistic structure and historical past. That's the way I approach the question of culture.

About Carlos Moore

Born in Cuba in 1942, Dr. Carlos Moore completed his doctoral and post-doctoral studies in ethnology at the University of Paris, France.

From 1975 to 1980, Moore lived in Dakar, Senegal, assisting Cheikh Anta Diop and acting as his personal interpreter.

A resident of Guadeloupe, he is currently Visiting Professor at Florida International University. In February, 1987, he convened the "First Conference on Negritude, Ethnicity, and Afro Cultures in the Americas" in homage to Aime Cesaire.